Brass Tacks
INTEGRATED SKILLS
IN ENGLISH

LYNNE GAETZ
Collège Lionel-Groulx

Prentice Hall Allyn and Bacon Canada
Scarborough, Ontario

Dedication

This book is dedicated to my students, and to my children Diego and Rebeka.

Canadian Cataloguing in Publication Data

Gaetz, Lynne, 1960-
    Brass Tacks Integrated skills in English

ISBN 0-13-760091-7

1. English language - Textbooks for second language.* 2. English
language - Problems, exercises, etc.   I. Title.

PE1128.G3274 1998 428.2'4 C97-930433-4

© 1998 Prentice-Hall Canada Inc., Scarborough, Ontario
A Division of Simon & Schuster/A Viacom Company

ALL RIGHTS RESERVED

Prentice-Hall, Inc., Upper Saddle River, New Jersey
Prentice-Hall International (UK) Limited, London
Prentice-Hall of Australia, Pty. Limited, Sydney
Prentice-Hall Hispanoamericana, S.A., Mexico City
Prentice-Hall of India Private Limited, New Delhi
Prentice-Hall of Japan, Inc., Tokyo
Simon & Schuster Asia Private Limited, Singapore
Editora Prentice-Hall do Brasil, Ltda., Rio de Janeiro

ISBN 0-13-760091-7

Acquisitions Editor: Dominique Roberge
Developmental Editor: Marta Tomins
Production Editor: Susan James
Copy Editor: Jean Ferrier
Proofreader: Allyson Latta
Production Coordinator: Jane Schell
Cover Design: Julia Hall/Zena Denchick
Interior Design: Zena Denchick
Page Layout: Phyllis Seto

Visit the Prentice Hall Canada Web site! Send us your comments, browse our
catalogues, and more. **www.phcanada.com** Or reach us through e-mail at
phabinfo_pubcanada@prenhall.com

    5   BBG   01 00 99 98

Printed and bound in the United States.

Table of Contents

Preface

Part 1 Skills

Chapter

Part 2 Grammar

Section

Preface

"Let's get down to brass tacks," a Cockney expression meaning "Let's get down to the basic facts," describes the approach that this book takes. Interesting and very "readable" essays are combined with helpful hints for the structuring of opinion essays. The second part of this book contains grammar exercises that should help you to improve your writing and speaking in English. *Brass Tacks* is recommended for intermediate level ESL and EFL students.

Brass Tacks contains essays and short stories by international writers. The essays in this book present a great variety of writing styles and themes. Dick Gregory describes a painful time in his childhood in the narrative essay "Shame" and Dorothy Nixon tells a humorous story about her family's attempt to give up television in "The Appalling Truth." Nobel Prize winner Pablo Neruda writes about an experience in his own backyard, Stephen King justifies the existence of horror movies and Hugh Garner and Gwynne Dyer look at fate and war respectively. Zlatko Dizdarevic's essay describing an incident in Sarajevo is a favourite among my students. The two short stories at the end of the reading section expose the students to fiction writing.

Each reading chapter contains vocabulary, reading comprehension and discussion questions. Writing and speaking suggestions are given at the end of each chapter. Teachers can use these ideas for homework assignments or for in-class testing. Chapters 9 and 10 contain controversial essays and any of these essays could be a launching pad for a research project or an organized formal debate.

In addition to exposing you to varied readings, this book also aims to help you structure your own writing. Chapters 1 to 9 contain Writing Tips sections. In these sections, rules for writing summaries and opinion essays are given in detail. You are also given the opportunity to practise various parts of the essay: the essay plan, the thesis statement and the topic sentence, the introduction, the conclusion and transitions between paragraphs. Chapter 9 contains hints on doing research in the Writing Tips section. Chapters 10, 11 and 12 contain Speaking Tips with a focus on planning debates, asking proper questions and preparing an oral opinion presentation.

In addition to units on the verb tenses, plurals, conditionals, and modals, the grammar section contains exercises on punctuating (comma, semicolon and quotation marks) and capitalizing. The two final units look at common spelling errors and gallicisms.

Appendices contain descriptions of parts of speech, gerunds and infinitives, and pronouns, as well as an exercise for each concept. In addition, there are communication activities for you to practice the structures you have learned, and a table of irregular verbs.

Each grammar unit contains clear explanations, so the grammar section could be used as a self-study manual. Any teacher who thinks that grammar is important, but doesn't have the time to explain grammar in class, could let you work at home in this book. Grammar could also be given prescriptively, with each of you doing only those chapters that relate to your own grammar problems.

Each grammar section contains some Class Exercises. The answers to these questions are not in the answer key because sometimes the teacher may want to explain a concept or do an exercise with you. Corrections to each numbered grammar exercise are in a separate answer key.

Now let's get down to *Brass Tacks*.

Acknowledgements

I would like to thank the following people for their help and support: my students, for letting me test this material with them, and the English Department at College Lionel-Groulx, especially Donna Canuel and Richard Pawsey. Many teachers generously tested the reading material and gave me valuable feedback, including Robin Dick, Heather Yorsten, Jean Philippe Lebonnois, Elizabeth Schinkle and Sonia Margossian. I am also indebted to Cliff Newman, Dominique Roberge, Marta Tomins, Marijke Leupen, Susan James, Nick Gamble and Jean Ferrier. I would like to thank Line Bechard, Jane Davey and Hugh Burgoyne for their encouragement, support and suggestions. I appreciate the useful comments from reviewers, in particular Geraldine M. Arbach, CEGEP de l'Outaouais, and Josephine Moffa, Collège de Maisonneuve. I would like to extend a special thanks to my parents, my husband and my children, who helped keep my spirits up and who put up with my long hours on the computer.

Serving the Senses

Essays come in a variety of shapes and sizes. More precisely, the term "essay" can encompass everything from the humor column in Saturday's paper to the serious condemnation of capitalism found in a political magazine. Essays can, among other things, inform us, persuade us to see things differently, tell us a story, describe an event, make us laugh or give us factual information.

Unlike the short story, the essay deals with subject matter that is, for the most part, nonfiction. While the short story is developed in the imagination of the writer, the essay is born in reality.

Most essay writing contains a certain amount of descriptive prose. With language, the writer is able to arouse our senses so that we can see, hear, smell, taste or feel what the writer is expressing. In the following essay, Montreal writer Joe Fiorito vividly describes a moment inside a Montreal smoked-meat restaurant.

Reading 1.1
Carnival of Carnivores
by Joe Fiorito

1   He had slick hair and dark eyes, the small man in the tired black suit. The woman with him was tall and hard and skinny, with long red nails she didn't use for typing. They walked into Schwartz's like bank robbers. Hungry for each other, I thought. Or maybe just him for her. It was high noon on a Friday.

2   I was having the usual, a regular smoked meat with fries and a black cherry soda. They took the seats at the end of the table. She sat stiffly and crossed her legs. No nylons. A guy notices these details.

3   The little man put his elbows on the table, leaned forward and whispered something quickly, softly to the woman. She didn't say a word, she didn't look at him. She looked around the room. But she heard what he said and she nodded.

4   The waiter came to discuss the menu, but there was no discussion. The little man knew what he wanted. The woman lit a smoke and fidgeted. When the little man looked at me, I smiled. I wanted to be sociable. His eyes were flat. The message was clear: mind your own business. I did.

5   When the woman was halfway through her cigarette, food started coming in waves. There was a large platter of regular smoked meat, with the bread on the side. A grilled steak, half a spiced chicken, and a couple of franks. A smoked meat on rye. Some grilled liver, and a couple of slices of veal.

6   The man took the sandwich and the fries.

7   The rest of the food was for her.

8   She parked her ultra-slim in the ashtray, took a deep breath and let it out with an all-in-a-day's-work sigh. She asked me for the ketchup. I gave it up without a word. I wasn't going to interfere with the little man's play. He didn't touch his sandwich. He wanted to watch her eat. That's what he was hungry for. She didn't disappoint.

9   She cut into her bloody steak and followed bites of it with bites of mustard-covered sausage. She salted her chicken and ate it with both hands. She laid strip after strip of smoked meat on her plate, swirled it in puddles of mustard and ketchup, and forked it into her mouth. The cigarette died slowly while she ate.

10   Schwartz's at lunch is always filled with cocky men whose badly fitting Boss suits are going shiny in the recession. They sit cheek-by-jowl with tattooed punks and whole tables of fat guys who spill out of baseball jackets and who order their smoked meat lean. Circulating among them are half a dozen elderly waiters with bald heads and white shirts, with pink faces and soft hands. Everyone stared at the woman.

11   The room was hushed. All of us wanted to sit where the little man sat. We wanted her to look at us the way she looked at her meat.

12   When she was done, she pushed her plate away and wiped her hands. She checked her lipstick with a pocket mirror and took a fresh cigarette. He lit it, but she didn't look at him. This was the ritual, a part of the game.

13   The waiter came and cleared the plates, smiled at her and left the bill. The little man with the slick hair studied the slip of paper. He double-checked the addition, and called the waiter back. The waiter had left some meat off the bill. It was an easy mistake. There'd been so much of it. The little man wanted to pay for everything he ordered. The woman stubbed her cigarette. Her nails shone redder than before.

14   They got up. She wore a grey skirt that hung loosely, as on a clothesline. You could see the bones of her hips when she moved. The sweater she wore was threadbare and clean. Her eyes were dull, as if she'd seen too much and none of it had impressed. She was anxious to leave.

15   Every man in Schwartz's wanted to leave with her.

VOCABULARY

When you do a lot of reading in a second language, it becomes very time consuming to constantly look up words in the dictionary. One way to learn the meaning of words is to look for *context clues*, which are words or phrases near the difficult word that give a hint about its meaning. When a word is read in context, you can guess what the meaning is, and most of the time you will be correct.

1. The man in "Carnival of Carnivores" is described in the first paragraph. "He had slick hair and dark eyes, the small man in the tired black suit." (para. 1) Without using your dictionary, find a synonym (word that means the same thing) for

   slick _____ *tired* _____

2. "The woman lit a smoke and fidgeted." (para. 4) Define *fidgeted*.

   _____

   _____

3. What is the meaning of *sigh*? Reread paragraph 8, and using the context clue   (the situation that she *sighs* in), try to define the word.

   _____

   _____

4. Find a word in paragraph 13 that means "to extinguish by crushing."

   _____

5. "The sweater she wore was threadbare and clean." (para. 14)
   What does *threadbare* mean?

   _____

   Is her sweater old or new?

   _____

READING COMPREHENSION

1. What was so interesting about the way the woman ate?

   _____

2. What do the waiters look like?

   _____

3. In paragraph 11 we learn that the room was *hushed*. Why was it hushed?

   _____

4. What role does the narrator (Joe Fiorito) play in events?

_____

5. In the text, highlight phrases that give the reader a clear picture of the female customer. In the lines below, briefly summarize what the female customer looks and acts like.

_____

_____

_____

6. **Who** is this essay about? _____

    Where does the action take place? _____

    When does the action occur? _____

    What happens? _____

    Why does it happen? _____

7. The **main idea** is the most important or central idea of a text. To find out the main idea of the essay, combine the answers to question 6 and restate them in one complete sentence.

_____

_____

_____

DISCUSSION

1. This text describes a moment in a particular place. It also creates a certain mood with the language. What words or phrases are particularly effective at arousing your senses?

2. Choose one or more of the following words to describe the author's attitude towards his material. Support your choice.
- serious
- amazed
- cynical
- critical
- curious
- detached

3. This text was written as one of a series of food essays and restaurant reviews, and it was originally published in Montreal's _Hour_ magazine. After reading the essay, do you feel like visiting Schwartz's restaurant? What differentiates this review from standard restaurant reviews?

# Writing Tips

The Topic Sentence

A good topic sentence introduces the subject of the paragraph and gets the reader's attention. The point that you are trying to make in your paragraph should be clearly evident in an interesting topic sentence. Everything else in the paragraph should be a detail that supports your topic sentence.

For example, if you write a paragraph about Uncle Fred, you could structure the paragraph as follows:

Topic sentence: *Uncle Fred is extremely accident prone.*

Details:
- *He often bangs his head on the door frame when he gets into his car.*
- *I've even seen him trip on the edge of our carpet.*
- *Last year he walked into a telephone pole and ended up with a huge bump on his forehead.*
- *The same day, he dropped a hammer on his toe.*
- *We try not to laugh at poor Uncle Fred, but he sure does hurt himself a lot.*

A good topic sentence is not too broad. Don't make your topic sentence so general that you need several paragraphs to support it.

I'm going to tell you everything about my uncle.
(This is impossible to do in one paragraph.)

A good topic sentence is not too narrow. The topic sentence should not be so specific that it is difficult to support it.

My uncle has brown eyes.
(What more is there to say about this topic?)

A good topic sentence unifies the paragraph. A topic sentence should be general enough that all of the details and examples in the paragraph relate back to it. Don't include facts in your paragraph that have nothing to do with the topic sentence. For example:

Topic sentence: *Uncle Fred is extremely accident prone.*

Detail: *My uncle has been married for fifty years.*
(The supporting detail really has nothing to do with the focus of the paragraph.)

WRITING TIPS EXERCISE 1

Read the following paragraph and identify the topic sentence (the sentence that unifies the paragraph). Then cross out any sentences that are not related to the topic sentence.

Sometimes we can blame the stinginess of wealthy adults on their memories of impoverished childhoods. In some cases we cannot be so generous. The American billionaire, Jean Paul Getty, was born with a silver spoon in his mouth, yet he was reputed to be one of the cheapest men in the world. Getty never had to worry about his next meal, and even when he got older, and left home, his first business ventures were financed by his wealthy oilman father. He was a very astute businessman, and he accumulated a fortune that surpassed that of his father. Yet in spite of the wealth, Getty was notoriously cheap. He married and divorced five times. In his large British estate he went to the trouble to install pay phones, because he worried that his guests might make long distance calls on his phone line. Getty owned Getty Oil Company. Even more remarkably, when his own grandson was kidnapped, Getty agreed to pay the ransom only after his grandson's ear was mailed to him in an envelope. Getty insisted at a later date that his grandson reimburse him for the ransom money! Getty accumulated art at one of his American homes. Surely no one has ever been more spectacularly cheap!

WRITING TIPS EXERCISE 2

In pairs, write a topic sentence for a paragraph that contains the following items: pantyhose, girdles, false eyelashes, high-heeled shoes, pointy-toed shoes. Ensure that your topic sentence gets the reader's attention and is not too broad or too narrow.

Writing Suggestions

1. Write a descriptive paragraph that focuses on one or more of the following senses.

   - smell
   - touch
   - taste
   - feeling
   - sight

   For example, you can describe your breakfast, your bedroom, someone's hands, or you can describe an intense feeling at a particular moment. Try to use interesting descriptive phrases, and use your dictionary or a thesaurus to come up with new vocabulary. Make sure that your paragraph has an interesting topic sentence.

2. Write a paragraph describing a friend or family member, or somebody who is famous. Write and highlight your topic sentence. Make sure that the rest of your paragraph is related to the topic sentence.

Speaking Suggestions

1. Informal Speaking Game

Find eight interesting and difficult vocabulary words (use your dictionary) that describe a famous person. Four of the words should describe the person physically, and four words should describe the person's character. Incorporate these descriptive words into a short paragraph about your famous person. Classmates guess who you are describing. If your classmates need more hints, they can ask you questions, but you can only answer "yes" or "no" to their questions. The person who guesses correctly must then present his or her paragraph.

2. Formal Speaking Presentation

Make a three- to five-minute presentation about someone whom you admire. Structure your presentation in the following way:

a) *Introduction* (background information). Who is that person and where is he or she from? What is that person's history? What admirable qualities does that person have?

b) *Give two reasons for admiring that person.* What specifically has that person done to deserve your respect? Give examples.

c) *Conclusion.* How has that person influenced your life? Make a suggestion to your audience, or make a prediction about that person.

For more information about preparing an oral presentation see Speaking Tips in Chapter 12.

Telling a Story

A narrative essay is a nonfiction composition that *tells a story*. The purpose in telling the story may be to illustrate a point, to entertain the reader or even to persuade the reader about something. The form of the narrative essay is consistent, however, and arises out of the writer's desire to express *what happened*.

The following narrative essay is by Pablo Neruda, the Nobel Prize-winning poet from Chile.

Reading 2.1

Friends All of US
by Pablo Neruda, translated by Robert Bly

1   One time, investigating in the backyard of our house in Temuco [Chile] the tiny objects and minuscule beings of my world, I came upon a hole in one of the boards of the fence. I looked through the hole and saw a landscape like that behind our house, uncared for, and wild. I moved back a few steps, because I sensed vaguely that something was about to happen. All of a sudden a hand appeared—a tiny hand of a boy about my own age. By the time I came close again, the hand was gone, and in its place there was a marvelous white sheep.

2   The sheep's wool was faded. Its wheels had escaped. All of this only made it more authentic. I had never seen such a wonderful sheep. I looked back through the hole but the boy had disappeared. I went into the house and brought out a treasure of my own: a pinecone, opened, full of odor and resin, which I adored. I set it down in the same spot and went off with the sheep.

3   I never saw either the hand or the boy again. And I have never again seen a sheep like that either. The toy I lost finally in a fire. But even now, in 1954, almost 50 years old, whenever I pass a toy shop, I look furtively into the window, but it's no use. They don't make sheep like that any more.

4 I have been a lucky man. To feel the intimacy of brothers is a marvelous thing in life. To feel the love of people whom we love is a fire that feeds our life. But to feel the affection that comes from those whom we do not know, from those unknown to us, who are watching over our sleep and solitude, over our dangers and our weaknesses—that is something still greater and more beautiful because it widens out the boundaries of our being, and unites all living things.

5 That exchange brought home to me for the first time a precious idea: that all of humanity is somehow together. That experience came to me again much later; this time it stood out strikingly against a background of trouble and persecution.

6 It won't surprise you then that I attempted to give something resiny, earthlike, and fragrant in exchange for human brotherhood. Just as I once left the pinecone by the fence, I have since left my words on the door of so many people who were unknown to me, people in prison, or hunted, or alone.

7 That is the great lesson I learned in my childhood, in the backyard of a lonely house. Maybe it was nothing but a game two boys played who didn't know each other and wanted to pass to the other some good things of life. Yet maybe this small and mysterious exchange of gifts remained inside me also, deep and indestructible, giving my poetry light.

VOCABULARY

1. Why do you think Neruda treasured a pinecone?

_____

2. "But even now, in 1954, almost 50 years old, whenever I pass a toy shop, I look furtively into the window, but it's no use." (para. 3) Without using your dictionary, guess the meaning of *furtively*.

_____

READING COMPREHENSION

1. Did Neruda know the boy next door? _____

2. Why was the young Neruda so touched by the gift of the sheep?

_____

_____

3. What did Neruda learn, and how did he learn it?

_____

_____

4. What effect does the young neighbor's gesture (giving the sheep) have on the rest of Pablo Neruda's life?

_____

_____

5. Write one sentence that sums up the central (main) idea of the text.

_____

_____

DISCUSSION

1. Did the boy who gave the sheep expect a present in return? Do most children give without expecting to receive? Do most adults give without expecting to receive?

2. What do you think a stranger would do if you gave him or her a gift for no reason?

Reading 2.2

First Steps
by Adele Berridge

1 When I was three years old, my mother worked for a brief period as a cosmetics saleswoman. She visited customers in their homes, and she brought along large cases filled with samples of the products. When I sat at the window watching her leave, I would marvel at how pretty she looked in her high heels, her little round hat and her pastel suits.

2 Our home was a typical suburban bungalow built in the 1950's. On the main floor, tucked into our linen closet, mom kept a large blue plastic box filled with about a hundred tiny lipstick samplers. My two brothers, my sister and I were repeatedly warned about touching mom's things. Yet... one sunny morning I found myself alone in the hallway in front of that linen closet. Mom was far away in the basement and I was feeling daring.

3 My little fingers opened the mysterious box filled with the tiny white tubes of lipstick. I *knew* that this cupboard was off limits to me. I could easily remember my mother saying "NO" in a sharp tone whenever I touched the box, but that day I felt like I was sleepwalking into danger.

4 I pulled off one lid and marveled at the red. It was such a glorious red, redder than any of my crayons. Redder than my brother's toy fire engine. No one saw or heard me, and I heard no footsteps coming, so I continued. The next lid came off and there was a bright purple stick, purple pink like my silly putty. I opened another, and another. Oranges, light pinks, even creamy whites. I didn't put the lipstick on me; I just wanted to look inside those smooth little tubes.

5   Then — far away — a door closed. Footsteps. Quickly I put the lids back on. My little fingers worked feverishly. Some lids squished the contents of their tubes. Lids were on. The blue box was closed just as those legs came towards me. My heart was pounding in my ears.

6   "Did you touch my lipsticks?" mom asked. Her white teeth clicked inside the red circle of a mouth. Which red, I wondered.

7   "No mommy." The lie was out. I looked her straight in the eye. A mysterious evil child was inhabiting me.

8   "Let me see your teeth!" my mother ordered. *My teeth*! I tried to open my lips but they wouldn't budge. She'll know, I kept thinking. She'll know. She always sees the lie when she looks at our teeth.

9   Not long after that incident I learned that the teeth test was a sneaky trick my mother played on us to convince us that lying somehow *showed*. I vaguely remember being scolded and sent to my room after the lipstick episode. Yet even with the punishment, even with the lectures, the importance of being honest was not yet a lesson that I could absorb.

10 Maybe two months later the next big incident occurred. My younger brother and I took an opportunity to investigate my older sister's bedroom while she was playing with a friend next door. On top of her dresser she had a scene of tiny ornaments. Most inviting was a delicate glass deer. I wanted to touch that deer, but it was up high. As my brother stood to the side watching, I pulled open the bottom drawer, and then the next drawer, until I made steps to the top of the dresser.

11 I had a little pair of running shoes on, and I climbed up, carefully stepping on the edge of each drawer. I was just reaching for the deer when the dresser started to tip towards me. Somehow I leapt off the drawer to safety just as the large piece of furniture crashed to the ground. In a split second, the glass ornaments smashed on the hardwood floor. My brother and I stared in stunned silence as hard footsteps clomped down the hall.

12 "Who did this?" mom shrieked, as my brother and I stood frozen with fear.

13 "He did it!" I assured her shamelessly, as my finger pointed at my quivering little brother.

14 The next minutes were a torrent of shouting, spanking, and loud wailing as my brother was punished for the act. I stood still, numb. Noises and colors swirled around me, the occasional image registering like a snapshot. As I walked back to my room in slow motion, I heard the distant sound of my brother's muffled sobs. At the time I knew that I was being *really, really bad*, but there was no turning back.

15 That incident has haunted me my whole life. My brother's tear-streaked red face is burned into my brain. I still see his disappointed eyes staring at me not with anger but with bewilderment. I was his sister, his best friend, and I had betrayed him in order to save myself. The guilt wouldn't go away. It was a constant presence during sleepless nights. Occasionally my brother would remind me of the incident and sometimes I even pretended that I couldn't remember that time, yet I *couldn't forget* it.

16 As a child I thought that the human soul was a round white pie plate and I imagined that sins were like black specks of dirt on it. In my mind's eye, my soul had been stained with the mud of sin. That incident planted a seed in me that budded and grew with time; I came to

realize that it's better to tell the truth and take responsibility for my actions than to lie and live with that horrible guilt. If I had simply told the truth and taken the punishment, most likely I wouldn't even remember the incident today. Because I lied, I've never forgotten it.

VOCABULARY

1. "I was feeling daring." (para. 2) What is *daring?* _____

2. What is the "teeth test?" (para. 8, 9) _____

3. Which of the following is the definition for the word *lecture*, as it is used in paragraph 9? _____
a. a discourse given before an audience
b. a reading
c. a speech intended to express disapproval

4. In paragraph 16 the narrator refers to her "soul." What is a *soul?* _____

Guess the meaning of the verbs in Column A by matching them with the possible definitions in Column B. Write the letter of the matching definition in the space provided. The number in parentheses indicates the paragraph where the verb can be found.

Column A			**Column B**
5. *tuck*	(2)	_____	**A.** to start to move
6. *squish*	(5)	_____	**B.** to jump high and far
7. *budge*	(8)	_____	**C.** to soil or discolor
8. *scold*	(9)	_____	**D.** to damage by pressing
9. *tip*	(11)	_____	**E.** to speak in a very loud voice
10. *leap*	(11)	_____	**F.** to hit on the buttocks with an open hand
11. *shout*	(14)	_____	**G.** to move in whirling confusion
12. *spank*	(14)	_____	**H.** to be treacherous to someone
13. *swirl*	(14)	_____	**I.** to put in a snug place
14. *betray*	(15)	_____	**J.** to rebuke angrily
15. *stain*	(16)	_____	**K.** to tilt or shift

READING COMPREHENSION

1. Who is this essay about?

_____

When do you think the events take place? Support your answer with information from the text.

_____

_____

Where does this essay take place?

_____

What does the narrator do in this text?

_____

_____

2. What does the narrator learn, and how does she learn it?

_____

_____

3. What is the **main idea** of this text? State the main idea in one sentence. Refer to your answers to questions 1 and 2 to help you.

_____

_____

_____

4. What is the tone of this essay? (*Tone* is the writer's attitude towards his or her material.) Choose one and then describe why you made that choice.

- reflective
- embarrassed
- sarcastic
- humorous
- angry
- detached

_____

_____

5. Find and highlight examples of descriptive writing in the text. What does this tell you about narrative writing?

_____

_____

DISCUSSION

1. When you were a small child, did your parents ever try anything like the "teeth test" on you?

2. "His disappointed eyes stared at me not with anger but with bewilderment." (para. 15) In your opinion, why did this have such an impact on the narrator?

3. Was the writer really an evil child? Explain.

4. What do the writer's references to *evil* and her *soul* tell you about her?

5. Could the writer have learned the lesson without the lie? Explain.

6. Can you identify with the writer of "First Steps"? Have you ever lied, or hurt someone, and then felt terrible about it afterwards?

riting Tips

The Summary

The focus of this chapter is the narrative essay. You will often be asked to describe something that you have seen, heard or read. The ability to summarize effectively then becomes important. The following instructions can help you summarize material you have read.

When you summarize a text, you select only the most important points and restate them in your own words. When you write a good summary, your ability to understand written material can be evaluated.

When preparing for a summary, look for:
- the reason the story was written
- repetitions of the same idea or theme
- the main characters, ideas or events
- the main problems, solutions

1. At the beginning of your summary, always identify the author and title of the work that you are summarizing.

2. Select only the main, essential ideas. Examples or details from the original work can be excluded. Preserve the order and emphasis of the original work.

3. Use your own words as much as possible.

4. If you do quote from the original work, put the quote in quotation marks. Not attributing quotes to the author is considered plagiarism.

5. Write about the author's opinions and experiences, and not your own.

WRITING TIPS EXERCISE

Summarize an article from a newspaper or magazine. You can present your summary orally, tape it or hand in a written copy, depending on your teacher's instructions.

Writing Suggestions

Choose one of the following topics and write a personal narrative essay. Your essay should be double spaced and should tell a true story about an event in your life.

1. Do something really kind for an acquaintance but don't explain why you're doing it. You don't have to spend any money. Your gift can be something homemade, or the gift can be with words or actions. *Don't expect anything in return.*

Write an essay about your "random act of kindness."
   - Describe what you gave.
   - Describe the circumstances of giving it (when, where and how).
   - Describe the outcome.
   - Did the exercise teach you anything?
   - How did you feel about it?

2. What life lessons have *you* learned? Write an essay describing an important event in your life that changed you and taught you a valuable life lesson. For example, have you ever insulted a friend, cheated at a game, picked on someone at school or done something really nice?
   - When, where and how did the incident unfold? How old were you?
   - What were your thoughts and feelings in connection with the incident?
   - How did the incident change the way you see or do things?

Speaking Suggestions

1. Play "Tell the Truth" to practice question formation, and correct use of the present perfect and the past tenses.

In groups of three, brainstorm about interesting or life-changing incidents that have happened to each of you. Then choose the most interesting story. In front of the class, each one of you must pretend that the story is true for you, even though it is really only true for one of you. The other two must answer your classmates' questions with lies.

For example:

   Bob, Carol and Ted decide to use Bob's story about getting arrested for dangerous driving. All three students begin by announcing to the class, "I have been arrested for dangerous driving."
   The class proceeds to question the three students in an attempt to find out who really did the dangerous driving. Carol and Ted lie about the event and the circumstances, but Bob tells the truth. After about ten minutes the class votes for the student that they believe is telling the truth.

There are other variations of this speaking game. Bob could tell three stories about himself, two which are true and one which is a lie. Other students in Bob's group must question Bob in an attempt to discover which story is the lie.

2. Make a more formal presentation before the group. Take one of the Writing Suggestions, and present your "act of kindness" experience or your life-changing experience orally.

In My Opinion

I n Chapter 1, Joe Fiorito tells a story about a woman who eats at Schwartz's, but his essay mainly gives a sensual impression of a place. In "First Steps," Adele Berridge's main purpose is to tell a story, but her essay contains descriptive prose. Therefore, the terms "descriptive essay" or "narrative essay" are not mutually exclusive.

In this chapter you will be reading and trying to write opinion essays. Opinion essays may contain description and some story telling, but their main purpose is to persuade the readers to agree with the author. These essays may even try to motivate the readers to take an action of some kind.

When you write your opinion essays, remember that the reader may not have the same point of view as you. It is important to back up your opinion with solid facts, quotes, examples, statistics or personal experiences.

Gwynne Dyer, a Montreal resident, has studied both war and human behavior for decades. In the following essay, he examines the possible effects of "children's entertainment" on our youth.

Reading 3.1 It's Called Children's Entertainment
by Gwynne Dyer

1   First, the good news. The pop psychologists were wrong: human beings *do* have a strong innate resistance to killing their own kind. The military have known about it for 50 years.

2   Now for the bad news. The military have developed techniques to overcome this resistance—but it's not only the military who are using them. All the industrialized societies are now unintentionally subjecting their children to the same techniques, with the same results.

3   We are teaching the kids to kill.

4   Where's the evidence? Even in the United States, after all, the murder rate has stayed roughly the same for the past 40 years.

5   But it has stayed the same despite a fivefold growth in the prison population since 1975, which presumably keeps a great many potential murderers off the streets.

6   Moreover, the rate of "aggravated assault" (defined as "assault with intent to kill or for the purpose of inflicting severe bodily injury by shooting, cutting, stabbing, maiming, poisoning, scalding, or by the use of acids, explosive or other means") has gone up *sevenfold* since 1955.

7   Prof. James Wilson of the University of California at Los Angeles estimates that with 1957-style medical services, the U.S. murder rate today would be three times higher than it is.

8   This is not just an American problem. The same steep rise in assaults has begun in most other developed countries, though often from a lower starting point. Elsewhere, too, it fails to translate into higher murder rates yet, but if current trends persist, it certainly will.

9   Something very bad is happening in the developed countries, and it is all our own stupid fault. That is the disturbing conclusion of Lt.-Col. Dave Grossman, a former paratrooper, trained psychologist and serving U.S. army officer.

10   Grossman, in a new book called *On Killing*, tries to dissect the nature of killing. He begins, as any soldier would, with what all military leaders and few civilians know: that you can train and arm a man, put him on the battlefield, and expose him to the imminent danger of death—and in most cases, he *still* won't kill.

11   Armies had been fighting battles for thousands of years before anybody realized this, for the non-killers were ashamed of their "cowardice" and didn't talk about it. It was only in the final years of World War II that U.S. army historians, conducting post-combat interviews with several hundred infantry companies under promise of anonymity, discovered that only 15 to 20 percent of the soldiers ever fired their weapons in battle.

12   The others didn't run away, but they couldn't bring themselves to kill another human being. And even the great majority of them who fired their weapons aimed high.

13   In fact, as few as 5 percent of the soldiers on the battlefield were doing almost all of the killing. This was a stunning revelation, but when the experts went back into military history, they discovered that it had always been true. They calculated the theoretical lethality of various kinds of weapons, and came up with kill rates 20 to 50 times higher than those actually observed in battle.

14   They found, for example, that 90 percent of the abandoned muskets picked up after the battle of Gettysburg (1863) were loaded but not fired—and almost half were double-loaded. A 19th-century soldier could not avoid the highly visible act of loading his musket, but nobody noticed if he didn't shoot it.

15   Naturally, the military promptly turned their attention to solving this "problem"—and they have succeeded. As Grossman points out, they solved it mainly by a combination of desensitization and conditioning techniques.

16   Soldiers no longer shoot at bull's-eyes; they train against pop-up targets resembling human beings in order to make shooting at human targets seem a familiar routine. They also undergo specific "operant conditioning," designed to make shooting so reflexive that they only have time to think about it afterward.

17   It worked so well that by the time of the Vietnam War, up to 95 percent of American soldiers were firing their weapons at the enemy—although, as Grossman points out, that is a large part of the reason why Vietnam veterans suffer such a very high rate of post-traumatic stress disease. They were effectively tricked into killing against their will.

18   But the point Grossman is leading up to is this: in the past 30 years, *for the first time*, we have unleashed almost identical techniques of desensitization and operant conditioning against our own children in the name of entertainment.

19   Only 20 years ago Sam Peckinpah's movies were the goriest thing around; now half the films on general release are bloodier. And the video arcades teem with games that are the precise equivalent of the military's operant conditioning. As Grossman puts it: "The same tools that more than quadrupled the firing rate in Vietnam are now in widespread use among our civilian population." With the results that we see all around us.

VOCABULARY

1. Find a word in paragraph 4 that means "about."

_____

2. Match the meanings of the following "aggravated assaults" (para. 6) with the definitions.

stabbing _____	a)	to burn with a hot liquid
maiming _____	b)	to wound by the thrust of a pointed weapon
scalding _____	c)	to mutilate or disfigure

3. The word *cowardice* means "disgracefully lacking in courage." Why did the author put the word in quotation marks in paragraph 11?

_____

4. The word *musket* appears in paragraph 14. Which phrase best defines a musket?___
a) a helmet, or head covering
b) a muzzle-loading military firearm
c) a bullet

5. Find a word in paragraph 18 that means "to let loose."

_____

READING COMPREHENSION

1. A musket is loaded through the open end of the weapon from which the bullet is discharged. In paragraph 14, the author states that almost half the guns picked up after the battle of Gettysberg were double-loaded. Why did those soldiers double-load their guns?

_____

2. Approximately what percentage of World War II veterans actually fired their guns in battle? _____ Of those who actually fired, did the majority of them kill someone? _____ What percentage of those soldiers on the battlefield were doing almost all of the killing? _____ What do these statistics tell you about human nature?

_____

3. According to the text, the military establishment has reacted to the fact that most soldiers can't kill easily. What techniques are now used to combat this "problem"?

_____

_____

4. What percentage of soldiers in the Vietnam War fired their weapons? _____ How were those soldiers affected?

_____

5. What is the main point that Gwynne Dyer is trying to make with this essay?

_____

_____

DISCUSSION

1. Are the author's arguments factual or emotional? Explain your answer.

2. Do any of the facts presented in this article surprise you? Which facts, and why?

3. Gwynne Dyer states in the text that "video arcades teem with games that are the precise equivalent of the military's operant conditioning." (para. 19) Do you agree with this statement? Explain.

4. Do you think that you, or your friends, have been influenced by violent movies or violent video games? Can you watch violent images without flinching?

Writing Tips

The Opinion Essay

In previous chapters you practiced writing descriptive paragraphs, and essays that tell a story. Now you will practice writing opinion essays.

An opinion is a judgment or belief, as opposed to fact. In the essay by Gwynne Dyer, he uses facts to support his belief that video games are training our youth to kill. A good opinion essay should state an opinion and use facts, statistics, examples and/or personal experiences to back up the opinion.

In opinion essays you need to convince the reader that your views are valid. Oral opinion presentations and opinion essays can have the following form:

Presentation of Opinion

The Introduction

In the introduction the reader's interest in the topic should be aroused. The thesis, or main point of the essay, should be mentioned in the introduction. A **thesis statement** is a general opinion statement, and the arguments that are in the body of the essay should provide the supporting reasons for the thesis statement.

The Body Paragraphs

Each body paragraph should back up the thesis statement with a clear reason. The point of each paragraph is expressed in a topic sentence. The topic sentence identifies the subject to be examined in that paragraph.

The paragraph should then be developed with **supporting facts and examples.** Remember, the facts and examples should be directly related to the topic sentence (focus sentence) of the paragraph.

The Conclusion

The concluding paragraph, which brings the essay to a satisfying end, can have the following form:

- Restate, but do not repeat the main points.
- End your conclusion with a prediction, suggestion or solution. The reader should be left with something to think about.

The Essay Plan

Before writing your essay, you should make an essay plan (outline). Your plan should have the following form:

Essay Plan (Outline)

Introduction	Anecdote, description or background information
	Thesis Statement:
	_____
	_____
Body 1	**Topic Sentence:**
	_____
	Supports: facts, examples, statistics or personal experiences:
	a) _____
	b) _____
Body 2	**Topic Sentence:**
	_____
	Supports: facts, examples, statistics or personal experiences:
	a) _____
	b) _____
Body 3	**Topic Sentence**
	_____
	Supports: facts, examples, statistics or personal experiences:
	a) _____
	b) _____
Conclusion	**Sum up** main points
	Give a final suggestion, prediction or solution

Sample Essay Plan—Violence in Movies

Introduction

Thesis Statement: Although some will argue that violent movies are simply a reflection of a violent society, I believe that these movies actually cause a lot of the violence around us.

Body 1

Topic Sentence: Violent movies are "how to" films for many sick individuals.

Supporting facts:

a) A well-known killer kept girls in a basement after seeing *Silence of the Lambs*

b) young couples have copied the heroes in *Natural Born Killers* and gone on killing sprees

Body 2

Topic Sentence: Violent movie heroes train children to solve problems with violence.

Supporting facts:

a) famous movie scene: Arnold Schwartzenegger divorces wife with machine gun; a generation of boys may copy him

b) in action movies, the heroes hurt people that they disagree with instead of talking through problems

Body 3

Topic Sentence: When movies were less violent, the world was less violent.

Supporting facts:

a) in past, women and children could walk on streets safely

b) old movies didn't focus on the machine gun as solution to all problems

Conclusion

Sum up: Violent movies train not only sick people, but all people how to solve problems violently, and ultimately those movies have made our world a more violent one.

Final suggestion: We could remove the profit from violent films by allowing victims of violence to sue movie producers each time someone acts out a scene from a violent movie.

Types of Arguments

Factual Arguments

A good opinion essay has a main point, or thesis, and arguments to support the thesis. Some arguments are based on researched facts and statistics.

Emotional Arguments

Sometimes writers attempt to sway the reader with arguments that appeal to the reader's emotions. Politicians, especially, often use emotional arguments to sway the public.

For example, during the Gulf War, stories about Iraqi soldiers throwing babies out of incubators inflamed the American public against Sadam Hussein. The stories were later found to be false, but the damage had been done, and support for America's involvement in the war grew.

What are some other examples where emotional arguments have been used to influence the public?

WRITING TIPS EXERCISE 1

1. Look again at the sample essay outline. Write F beside the arguments that you think are probably going to be factual, and write E beside arguments that are emotional. Some arguments can be factual, and appeal to the emotions as well.

2. A lot of the arguments in the sample essay outline would be very weak without some supporting proof, such as a quote from a respected source. Look at Gwynne Dyer's essay "It's Called Children's Entertainment" again, and highlight examples in the article where a source for factual material is mentioned.

WRITING TIPS EXERCISE 2

Gwynne Dyer's essay is a good example of an opinion essay. Although he doesn't follow the five-paragraph essay plan that you will be using, his essay is very structured. See if you can follow Gwynne Dyer's logic by answering the following questions.

1. In the introductory section to the Gwynne Dyer article, the main point of the essay is stated. What is the main point (thesis) of this essay?

_____

_____

2. Gwynne Dyer develops his argument with three points. For each of the following points, find two supporting facts or examples.

a) *The violent crime rate is increasing.*
Supporting facts or examples:

_____

_____

b) *Historically humans cannot easily kill each other.*
Supporting facts or examples:

_____

_____

c) *The military have solved the problem with desensitization and conditioning techniques.*
Supporting facts or examples:

_____

_____

3. What is the concluding point?

_____

_____

Writing Suggestion

Write an opinion essay about one of the following subjects. Remember to make an essay plan.

1. Violent video games desensitize teenagers
2. Violent video games should/should not be banned
3. Humans are inherently violent

Speaking Suggestion

Find a short article about any controversial subject. In a presentation of about five minutes do the following:

1. Briefly summarize the article. Remember to mention the name of the author and the title of the article. Also mention the name of the book, magazine or newspaper where you found the article. Make sure you summarize the article's main points, and not each and every detail.

2. Give two reasons, with supporting examples, for why you agree or disagree with the author's thesis. If you agree, support your opinion with your own arguments. Do not simply repeat what the author said, and do not pass off the author's arguments as your own.

3. Conclude by briefly restating your main points, and make a prediction or suggestion.

If the teacher wants to practise question formations, other students in a group could ask the presenter questions about the topic.

A War Story

Most of us will likely never have to experience life on a battlefield, but we do receive images of fighting on our televisions. As we hear of distant wars, buildings, looking like toy blocks, blow up on our screens.

It is easy to forget that war involves flesh and blood humans who get tired, hungry, cranky and lonely. In his book, *Portraits of Sarajevo*, Zlatko Dizdarevic, editor-in-chief of a celebrated Sarajevo newspaper, captures the experiences of soldiers on the front line.

In the following essay, Dizdarevic tells a story about a soldier who lived through battles on Zuc Mountain, a place of legend in the siege of Sarajevo. The mountain, which was once covered with forests and meadows, has become a wasteland, devastated by bombs and shells.

Reading 4.1 # Where Are You Going, Kid?
by Zlatko Dizdarevic

1 I heard the following story from a student named Salko Huntic. He was in the final hours of a three-day leave from fighting in the trenches on Zuc Mountain, and told me the story while sipping a beer at a café in Sarajevo.

2 It happened one day at the beginning of winter. There was a light mist in the air. My buddy and I were on guard duty when a boy, ten or 12 years old, appeared through the underbrush. When he caught sight of us, he froze, obviously frightened. He quickly tried to retrace his steps but found it was impossible. On his arm was a wicker basket covered with a white cloth.

3 "Where are you going, kid?" we asked. "Are you looking for somebody?"

4 "I'm going to see my father," he said. "My mother sent me with his lunch and some socks for tonight. She says he'll be cold without them."

5 The boy was so terrified he could barely talk.

6   "And where is your father?" we asked. "Do you know where to find him?"

7   "I don't know," he quavered. "I thought he'd be near here. I went the way my mother told me, but maybe I got lost."

8   "What's your father's name?"

9   "Jovo."[1]

10   "Well, you must know that your father can't be here," we told the boy. "He must be over there, on the other side."

11   The boy started to cry, clutching the basket in his cold hands. He repeated softly that his mother would kill him if she knew he'd got lost. So I stood up in the trench and called through the mist towards the enemy lines:

12   "Jovo! Your son is over here! Can you hear me?"

13   All was silent for a minute, then a voice came back:

14   "I don't believe it. You're lying to get me out of the trench."

15   "No, we just wanted to tell you not to shoot. The boy is coming across to bring you your lunch."

16   I told the boy not to be afraid, but to run over to the other side and come back the same way: That way he wouldn't get lost. I could see that he didn't really believe us. Still, he got out of the trench and began running to the other side. At one point, the white cloth fell off the basket. He took a few strides, stopped to think, then came back. He picked up the muddied cloth and ran to where his father's voice had come from.

17   For a long time, an hour or two maybe, we heard nothing. Just silence. They didn't fire, and neither did we. Suddenly Jovo's voice, which we now recognized, came out of the mist:

18   "The boy would like to come back now. You won't shoot, will you? He wants to go home."

19   "Okay," we answered.

20   Strangely, I looked forward to seeing the boy, who would probably be less frightened than before.

21   Suddenly he came out of the mist and hurried down into our trench. The basket was full. There was a bottle stoppered with a wad of old newspaper, a few apples and a piece of cheese.

22   "Here," said the boy. "My father sends you this. You can eat and drink a little. But he would like to ask for two cigarettes, if you have any. He hasn't seen a cigarette in three days."

23   *This was going a bit too far*, I thought to myself. The boy looked at me and my buddy as if he had something else to say, but he hesitated.

24   "Go on, kid," I urged him. "Did your father tell you anything else?'

25   "He said to tell you that he's leaving here tomorrow, and that they won't shoot tonight. If you agree, everyone can get some sleep. He said that others will relieve them tomorrow, and they will shoot a lot. They are not from around here."

[1] In former Yugoslavia, names usually reveal a person's ethnic origin, e.g., Bosnian Muslim, Serb or Croat.

26   We tied a stone to a pack of cigarettes. I stood up in the trench and yelled into the mist:

27   "Jovo, catch these! As for tonight, we agree, so long as we can trust you."

28   "We'll forget about standing watch for tonight," he replied. "You can do the same if you want, and we'll see who keeps their word. Thanks for the boy and for the smokes."

29   They didn't shoot that night, and neither did we. Around noon the next day, all hell broke loose: Bursting shells shook the air and the land.

30   I never saw the boy again, and Jovo never again spoke to us across the mist. But I will remember them to the end of my days.

VOCABULARY

1. The boy "appeared through the underbrush." (para. 2) What is the *underbrush*?

_____

Each of the following words can be defined in several ways. Find the word in the paragraph (paragraph number is indicated in parentheses) and decide which definition is closest in meaning to the way the word is used in the story. Circle the letter of the appropriate definition.

2. *quavered* (para. 7)
   a) a vibrating sound
   b) to tremble or shake
   c) to hesitate

3. *clutch* (para. 11)
   a) to grasp or hold tightly
   b) a nest of eggs
   c) cruel or unrelenting control

4. *stride*s (para. 16)
   a) a step, or the distance covered by a step
   b) a stage of progress in research
   c) to part the legs wide and sit on something

5. *wad* (para. 21)
   a) a roll of paper money
   b) a plug used to retain powder in a gun
   c) a small bundle of something pliable

6. Find the expression in paragraph 29 or 30 that means "there was total pandemonium."

_____

What expression in your language means the same thing?

_____

READING COMPREHENSION

1. In your opinion, why was the little boy safe as he ran back and forth across the battlefield?

_____

_____

2. In paragraph 20, the narrator says, "Strangely, I looked forward to seeing the boy..." Why did he feel that way?

_____

_____

3. Why did the soldiers keep their word about not shooting during the night? It would have been easy for one side to attack the other.

_____

_____

4. What impact did that little boy have on the soldiers in both trenches?

_____

_____

5. In a sentence, what is the **main idea** of this text?

_____

_____

DISCUSSION

1. This story depicts a war fought "in the trenches." How is this type of fighting different from the type of fighting we saw on our TV screens during the Gulf War?

2. During the Gulf War many soldiers simply fired, from the air, at ground targets. Do you think that it is psychologically easier to fight this type of battle than to fight in trench warfare? Which type of fighting is more dehumanizing?

3. What do you know about the war in Bosnia? Share your knowledge.

4. Is there any circumstance where you would consider fighting in a war?

5. Have any wars been started for a just, or honorable reason? Can you think of any valid reason for starting a war?

# Writing Tips

The Thesis Statement

The thesis statement is a statement of opinion, and it identifies the subject of the essay. It is unnecessary to refer to yourself in the thesis statement. Phrases like "I believe" or "I am going to talk about" are superfluous.

In reports or research papers it is useful to let the reader know immediately what your arguments are going to be. However, in opinion essay writing, this removes the punch from subsequent paragraphs. Therefore, in opinion essays, simply state your opinion in the thesis, and leave your main points for the body of the essay.

Supporting the thesis statement

A thesis statement must be supported with clear reasons. Each reason becomes the focus of a supporting paragraph.

> Although smokers will complain that their freedom is being curtailed, smoking should be banned from all public places.

- Tobacco-related health care costs
- Second-hand smoke
- Majority support smoking ban
- Create "smoking centres"

WRITING TIPS EXERCISE 1

Most of the following thesis statements are weak. Analyze and then edit them. Which thesis statement is the best?

1. In my essay I'm going to convince you that hockey has become too violent.
2. Hockey violence is really just destroying the artistry of the game because superb scorers have to constantly worry about being attacked by the opposing teams' goons.
3.. I believe that hockey is becoming too violent, and something should be done about it.
4. Ice hockey, which could be a celebration of the players' artistry and skill on the ice, has deteriorated into a brutal and violent sport.

Look at the following topics and then, on a separate piece of paper, create interesting thesis statements.

1. It's better to live in Canada (or in the U.S.)
2. Censoring the Internet
3. Spanking of children
4. Banning violent video games
5. Capital punishment
6. Killing animals for their fur
7. Society's obsession with beauty
8. The greatest movie of all time is…

WRITING TIPS EXERCISE 2

Look at your thesis statements from Writing Tips Exercise 1. Choose your best thesis statement, and brainstorm at least three supporting arguments for your thesis.

The Topic Sentence

An essay generally contains several supporting paragraphs, and each paragraph has a main idea. The main idea of the paragraph is expressed in the topic sentence.

In the previous example, four supporting arguments are listed, but they are not topic sentences. To make them into topic sentences they must be made into strong, interesting statements.

Supporting Idea	Topic Sentence
Second-hand smoke	There is irrefutable evidence that smoke from cigarettes damages the lungs of non-smokers who are in the vicinity.

The topic sentence should provide relevant support for the thesis statement.

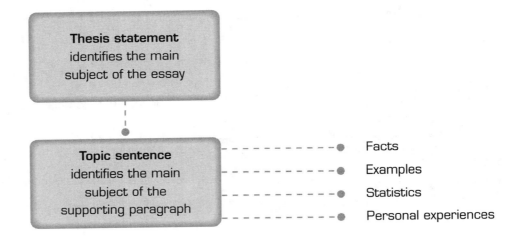

WRITING TIPS EXERCISE 3

Look at your supporting reasons for your thesis statement, and now make them into interesting topic sentences.

WRITING TIPS EXERCISE 4

Read the following short essay. Highlight the thesis statement in the introduction, and highlight the topic sentence in each supporting paragraph.

Butt Out!

(Introduction) Every noon hour I head to our student cafeteria to eat my lunch. As soon as I enter the room I notice the cloud of smoke hovering near the ceiling. I generally order a soup, and I sit near the door. Cigarettes dangle from the fingers of my peers, and one person after another casually exhales toxic fumes. The hovering haze of smoke thickens. The sickening smell of nicotine mixes with the flavor of my soup and I am left to eat, drink, inhale and absorb the tar and nicotine of countless cigarettes. Although smokers will complain that their freedom is being curtailed, smoking should be banned from all public places.

(First support) I do not play loud music in public because I am aware that I may damage the eardrums of others. We can't ride motorscooters inside malls because the exhaust fumes make other people feel sick. We would never cough or sneeze on someone's plate of food, because such a disrespectful act could damage that person's health. Why should smokers have the right to pollute our air? People who smoke in public places show a complete lack of respect for those around them, and such disrespect should not be tolerated.

(Second support) Furthermore, there is irrefutable evidence that second-hand smoke damages the lungs of non-smokers. When tobacco companies are willing to admit that cigarettes harm non-smokers, you can be sure that the evidence is rock-solid. My aunt recently died after a prolonged battle with lung cancer, yet she had never smoked a cigarette. She lived with my uncle, a chain smoker, and because of his addiction to nicotine, my aunt's life was cut short. Smokers in the past weren't aware of the damage that they were causing to others, but no smoker today can claim such ignorance.

(Third support) Every day people enter government-funded hospitals with emphysema, heart problems and cancer. All of us pay the price for a society that permits smoking indoors, because smoking-related illnesses use up a large percentage of our health-care dollars. A smoking ban will improve the condition of both our health and our wallets.

(Conclusion) As soon as smoking is banned in all public places, we will see the benefits. Our hospitals will treat fewer smoking-related illnesses, and this will save money. Non-smokers will be saved from noxious fumes, and smokers, who will be forced to smoke outdoors, might feel a greater desire to give up the habit. In the future, I hope that a non-smoker can go through life without having to breathe in someone else's cigarette smoke.

WRITING TIPS EXERCISE 5

Read the following essay. After you have finished reading the essay, do the following:

1. Create an effective **thesis** (opinion) **statement.** The thesis statement sums up the point of the entire essay.

2. At the beginning of each body paragraph write **topic sentences**. The topic sentence should sum up the main point of the paragraph in an interesting way.

Women on the Road

(Introduction) It really is wonderful to be a woman at this point in history. I feel like I can do just about anything that a man can do. If my female ancestors could see me now, they would be amazed. When my grandmother was young, she could not go to the next city without a male companion. My own mother was discouraged from going on a trip across Canada with friends. I, as a single young woman, have managed to travel to over twenty countries *alone*, and I have had a safe and exciting time doing it.

Thesis Statement: _____

_____

_____

(Body 1) Topic Sentence: _____

_____

_____

I will give you an example. When I arrived in India, at first I wore my usual warm weather clothing. Everywhere I went, I seemed to attract attention. As a woman on her own I was vulnerable, and extra attention was not exactly what I wanted. I was in a country where most people bathe fully dressed, yet I was walking around in short shorts and a half top with spaghetti straps. My life became considerably more peaceful when I began to dress like the local women. I could blend in and do my daily activities almost unnoticed. Besides, it was taken as a sign of respect towards the local culture when I dressed in traditional clothing.

(Body 2) Topic Sentence: _____

_____

_____

Hitchhiking is a little too much like Russian Roulette. Also, do not walk on streets alone in the middle of the night. When a situation feels uncomfortable, leave. When a place gives you a bad feeling in the pit of your stomach, calmly get away from there. That little voice inside you is sometimes all the protection you have.

(Body 3) Topic Sentence: _____

_____

_____

Humans are like dogs: they smell fear. You must walk with a confident gait, look straight ahead, and, most important, do not look away if someone stares at you in an intimidating way. Look at that person long enough to let him know that *you know he is looking, and it does not bother you a bit.* Your face can be neutral, and your gaze should linger only long enough to let him know that you see him looking and you don't like it. I have given strange men a *"don't mess with me!"* stare if I thought they deserved it. I am a small woman, yet I discovered in myself a very strong survival instinct. I knew I *could not* be afraid.

(Conclusion) Although there are certain risks inherent in a solo voyage, it is an experience that is unforgettable. In my years of traveling and working in foreign countries, I've never been hurt physically, and I have only been robbed once. (On a Paris metro, a pickpocket stole about two dollars from me.) Of course, a little common sense is necessary and, as I have pointed out, certain precautions can be taken to avoid problems, such as dressing like the locals do and avoiding situations that are clearly dangerous. If you decide to make a trip to a foreign destination, alone, I am sure that you will never regret the experience.

Writing Suggestion

Choose one of the following topics and write an essay plan for that topic. Your plan should follow the essay plan form described in Chapter 3. You do not have to write the entire essay, but you should have a complete thesis statement, three complete topic sentences and two supporting points for each topic sentence.

1. It's better to live in Canada (or in the U.S.)
2. Censoring the Internet
3. Spanking of children
4. Banning violent video games
5. Capital punishment
6. Killing animals for their fur
7. Society's obsession with beauty
8. The greatest movie of all time is…

Speaking Suggestion

Present your opinion on any of the topics listed in Writing Suggestions. You should introduce your topic, come up with at least three supporting reasons, and have a conclusion.

The Appalling Truth

When we surrender ourselves to something in an obsessive way, we consider ourselves addicted. Certainly, no one takes the addiction to gambling, drugs, food or alcohol lightly. In these cases, a person's quality of life, or even life itself, can be destroyed.

In recent years, the term "addiction" has been used in a more casual way. There are those who complain that they are hooked on chocolate, books or a certain song. In these cases, the term refers to the tendency to focus on a pleasurable activity. At what point does the pursuit of pleasure become a full-blown addiction?

Dorothy Nixon, a native Montrealer, is a free-lance writer and mother. In the following essay she looks at her family's addiction to the television.

Reading 5.1 ## The Appalling Truth
by Dorothy Nixon

1 Technology changes us. With the invention of the clock we have lost the ability to live in the present. The telephone has made us slaves, in the Pavlovian sense, to a ringing bell. With the advent of television we all moved indoors, leaving the streets empty and clear for the criminal element, and we left our minds open and susceptible to the mash served up on the screens.

2 As a mother and very serious media watcher, I am as troubled as anyone about the violent and sexist content on television. But were television wall-to-wall PBS type programming, without commercials, I would be just as concerned. I just don't like what it is doing to my family. It has become some kind of oracle — never mind McLuhan's "electronic fireplace"—it commands all of our attention and we don't listen to each other: husband to

wife, parents to kids, kids to parents. It was with this in mind that I suggested to my husband that we ban the tube from the house, on an experimental basis, for, say, about a year.

3   "No way!" he said.

4   "Why not?" I asked.

5   "Because, it would be hypocritical," he deftly answered. "We both work in the TV industry."

6   "You work in TV. I don't," I countered.

7   "Well, you like to *criticize* TV for the local paper. How can you criticize something you don't watch?"

8   "Good point."

9   "I just don't like what that thing is doing to our family," I continued. "It's noisy. It jangles the nerves. It's like a drug. It's addictive. We watch anything, anything, even Friday night programming. I mean, I used to read Dostoyovesky. Now I watch Steve Erkle! Besides, the stupid contraption keeps us from doing what human beings are really supposed to be doing."

10   "What's that? Foraging for nuts and berries?" My husband, the TV junkie, sees nothing wrong with the boob tube. "I grew up on TV and I'm no psycho." If my husband had his way there would be a TV in every room. And they'd all be tuned in to *Star Trek*. And, I must admit, there are times when I felt the only interest we had in common was *Star Trek* or *ER*. In the early months of my first pregnancy we'd cuddle together on the couch like two spoons and I'd fall asleep, head cradled in his lap, eyes on the tube. Togetherness.

11   But now we're like two channel-zapping zombies. "You know, *they* say that spending time together in front of the television does nothing to enhance a relationship." I tell my now bleary-eyed husband, trying to make him feel guilty. It's a war of attrition and it is working, sort of.

12   "OK. Two weeks," my husband relents. "We'll try no TV for two weeks. That's all. But *you* tell the kids." We have two boys, Andrew and Mark, 7 and 4. They kick up a huge fuss when I tell them that our tiny bungalow has been unilaterally declared a TV free zone. Now it's their turn to try to make me feel guilty. They hang their pathetic little heads in genuine mourning as they watch their dad reluctantly disconnect the enormous tangle of wires enabling the miracle of modern home theatre in our suburban castle. And am I feeling guilty? No way! I stand tall and victorious in our living room, the protector of my children.

13   That evening, we read our children books, sing them songs and tuck them in for the night. I go to bed with that Margaret Drabble I've been using as a giant paper-weight for the past year and my husband snuggles up with Stephen King.

14   Two days pass. The kids have finally stopped complaining about their terrible loss. In fact, they don't appear to care at all, anymore. They have found other, more interesting things to do. I, on the other hand, am suffering from a mean case of withdrawal.

15   "It's *Seinfeld* night and it's the *only* show I like. Do you think maybe you can bring the TV up for just this show?" I ask my husband, who happens to be down in his workroom drilling

a hole into a six foot piece of plywood for no apparent reason. "We'll keep the sound really low"... (because kids can hear hypocrisy even in their sleep.)

16   "Why don't you read, Ms. Literature Freak? You haven't exactly been burning up the library shelves," my husband sneers, rather condescendingly as he stops to wipe some sawdust from his nosehairs.

17   "Well, that's because I only read the best, and my brain's too fried at the end of the day to read the best," I answer, convincing even myself. (That has been my pat excuse for my intellectual lethargy since becoming a mother.)

18   My husband rolls his eyes and puts down the drill. No further argument from him. He happily carries the TV upstairs and reconnects the myriad wires in no time. We sit back and laugh at George and Kramer, Elaine and Jerry. The problem is, we do the same for *Murphy Brown* a few days later. And for *Friends*. Each night my husband clambering up the basement stairs with a 20 inch Sony stuck to his face, and then stumbling down again thirty-something minutes later, trailing his wires behind him.

19   Then the true test. Indeed, a real dilemma for us. A brand new *Star Trek* is airing, but at 7:00, before the kids' bed time. What to do? Clearly no sleazy hypocritical way around this.

20   "I can always get a tape and watch it at work," my husband, the news editor, smiles, taunting me once again. "You, on the other hand, will have to do without."

21   A real dilemma, yet I am not alone in my obsession. I recall a friend, a fortyish, married with two kids type, unapologetically telling me that watching *Star Trek* was the highlight of his day. "It's the only *philosophical* show on TV," he claimed.

22   And certainly, here is the new captain of the starship, perhaps the wisest person in the universe, forcing me to face a very ugly personal truth: It isn't my kids; it isn't even my husband. I am the real TV addict in my household. For, as my husband likes to point out, if the holodeck really existed, who would bother spending time anywhere else?

VOCABULARY

1.   "Television has become some kind of oracle." (para. 2) What do you think the author means?

_____

2.   What is "the boob tube"? (para. 10)

_____

3.   "They hang their pathetic little heads in genuine mourning." (para. 12) From the context, guess the meaning of *mourning*.

_____

4.   Find a word in paragraph 16 that means "scornful facial expression."

_____

5. Originally, the television was intended to provide us with a pleasurable leisure-time activity. Is the term "addiction" appropriate in this essay? Why or why not?

_____

_____

READING COMPREHENSION

1. The narrator wants to remove the TV from her home. What are five reasons that she gives?

a) _____

b) _____

c) _____

d) _____

e) _____

2. What is the narrator's tone? Choose one (or more), and defend your choice.
   • didactic   • solemn   • curious   • cynical   • lighthearted   • detached

_____

_____

3. Why does the narrator ultimately return the television to its roost?

_____

_____

DISCUSSION

1. What are some things that you feel addicted to? Brainstorm about activities that focus your attention in your free time.

2. Why do people become addicted to things? What are they looking for, or what are they trying to escape?

3. Is television addiction a serious problem? Why or why not?

4. Was the television a focal point in your family's home? Have your parents ever limited your television viewing, or banned it altogether?

5. When you have children, will you restrict their television viewing? Why or why not?

6. When does the pursuit of pleasure become a full-blown addiction?

Writing Tips

Reviewing a Show (Film, Play or Television Show)

When you watch a movie, a play, or a television show, most likely you simply tell your friends that the show is "great" or "bad." If your teacher asks you to review a show, you must be able to deliver a more thorough explanation of what *makes* the show worth watching.

The Elements in a Review

When reviewing a show for an oral or written presentation, you should include the following elements:

1. Introduction

Begin with an anecdote, background information or a description of a scene. Write a clear thesis statement that contains the name of the show that you are reviewing, and gives your opinion about that show. Do not give reasons for your opinion in your introduction.

2. Body

Support your opinion about the show with three well-developed supporting ideas. You may refer to any three of the following:

- acting
- characters
- script
- setting
- message
- special effects
- music
- humor

These elements are described in more detail in the section that follows.

3. Conclusion

Briefly restate your thesis, and your main reasons for your opinion, and end with a recommendation. You could give the show a rating out of five stars.

The Body — Reasons for Your Opinion

Your review of a show must be supported with three reasons. You can choose to analyze any three of the following elements.

Make sure you provide **supporting examples** for each element you examine.

1. Acting

In an analysis of the acting in a show, make sure that you make a distinction between the real human being who is playing the role, and the character that the actor portrays. You may hate a character in a movie, but still appreciate the terrific acting.

When analyzing acting, ask yourself the following questions:

a) Is the actor convincing?

b) Does the actor have a lot of experience? (You could refer to previous roles.)

c) Has the actor done a better job in other roles?

d) Were the main actors well cast? For example, some people believe that Michael Keaton was miscast as Batman because he doesn't have the physical build or the dark spirit to convincingly portray the tortured superhero. Ask yourself if the actors fit their roles.

Provide an example from the show to support your point. For example, if you think that John Travolta is a good actor, simply saying that he is great won't convince your audience. Give examples of scenes, or various roles, that show his great acting range.

2. Characters

The actors portray characters on screen. For example, the actor Sylvester Stallone played the character "Rocky" on film. You may dislike an actor such as Sylvester Stallone, yet be interested in a character he portrays.

When analyzing character, ask yourself the following questions:

a) Are the characters realistic? interesting?

b) What are the main character's morals? ambitions?

c) Does the character change during the show? Does the character learn something about him- or herself?

d) How does the character add to the script? Is the show mainly about the character (as in *Forrest Gump*) or do characters take a back seat to the action (as in *Independence Day*)?

3. Script

The essays that you write have a certain structure, including an introduction, a body and a conclusion. Most scripts also contain a sequence of events that are arranged in a specific way.

When you analyze the script, look at the way that the story is structured, and give your opinion about the structure.

a) Introduction   What is the situation at the beginning of the story? Is everything harmonious? Is tension already evident between the characters?

b) Rising Action   In most stories the action "rises" when a conflict occurs. The conflict leads to increased tension in the story. What incident happens to complicate events?

Does the main character enter into a conflict with:

- other characters? (*Braveheart*)
- with the environment? (*Twister*)
- with himself or herself? (In *The Godfather*, Al Pacino's character struggles against his own decent and honest nature as he slowly gets drawn into his family's crime business.)

There may be more than one type of conflict.

c) Climax What scene is the high point that changes the entire course of events? This scene resolves the major conflict in the film. For example, in the film *Independence Day* the climax occurs when the alien spaceship is destroyed, and we realize that humans will survive.

d) Conclusion How do the loose ends of the story tie up? Does everyone live happily ever after? Are we left hanging (in preparation for a sequel)?

4. Setting

All stories are situated in a time, place and culture. You may love a film mainly because you enjoy the period of time and the cultural context of the story.

In order to analyze setting, think about the following points:

a) When does the story take place? What is the time span?

b) Where does the story take place? (country, city, neighborhood)

c) What is the cultural context (social, economic and political) of this story? For example, in the television show *The Wonder Years*, the setting is an element that makes the show interesting. The show is situated in an American town in the late 1960s, and political and social movements of that period are often depicted.

Your argument would be weak if you simply say that the setting is interesting. Provide an example to back up your point.

5. Message

In a lot of stories the message is very black and white; the good guys win and the bad guys lose. However, in some scripts, the message is one of the most interesting aspects of the story. The film *Schindler's List* is poignant because of the complex, thought-provoking moral.

When analyzing message, ask yourself the following questions:

a) Why was the story written? What message did the writer want to convey?

b) What does the show tell you about human nature?

c) Do you think about the issues raised in the show long after it is over?

6. Special Effects/Music/Humour

Some films are great mainly because of the fantastic special effects. (Remember the dinosaurs in the movie *Jurassic Park*?) Other films have musical soundtracks that are memorable. Finally, some movies have no message, and very little story, yet you always remember them because they are so funny.

WRITING TIPS EXERCISE

Before reviewing a show, see if you can match the following vocabulary words with their meanings. Put the letter of the definition in the space provided.

_____ **1.** The producer

_____ **2.** The director

_____ **3.** The comedian

_____ **4.** The set

_____ **5.** Stuntman and stuntwoman

_____ **6.** The casting director

_____ **7.** The extras

_____ **8.** The editor

A. is a place (house, room…) where the action is filmed

B. chooses what actors will appear in the film

C. finances the film

D. appear in the background of scenes

E. makes the audience laugh

F. tells the actors what to do in a scene

G. cuts the film and decides what scenes to keep

H. do dangerous scenes so that the highly-paid main actors won't get hurt.

Writing Suggestions

1. Write a short essay on one of the following topics:
   a) My life without television.
   b) Television addiction is a serious problem.
   c) The pursuit of pleasure becomes an addiction when…

2. Watch an English-language television show that tells a story (no news or sports events) and write a review of that show. Make sure to plan your essay before writing it.

Your review will be most effective if you review a show that you feel quite passionate about. Remember that you can also review a show that you absolutely hate; just make sure that you can back up your opinion with solid facts and examples.

In your essay, you can analyze any three components of the show. Refer to the previous section entitled The Body — Reasons for Your Opinion.

Speaking Suggestion

Review a movie that you have a strong opinion about. To successfully prepare and present your talk, follow the steps listed in the Writing Tips section.

To support one of your points you could show a one-minute film clip. Make sure that the scene you choose to show supports one of your points. For example, if you like the acting, show us a scene in which the actors shine. If you hate the music, show us a particularly terrible song.

Make sure that you do not read your movie review. Use cue cards. For more information about preparing for an oral presentation, see Speaking Tips: Oral Opinion Presentations, in Chapter 12 of this book.

# In Defence of Horror Films

Since the birth of movies, the horror film genre has existed. Early audiences fainted at the sight of King Kong or Frankenstein. Since then, we've seen men turn into flies, and the dead climb out of graves. One thing is certain: horror movies have always been both fascinating and repulsive.

Stephen King has become a wealthy man because of our fascination with horror movies and horror stories. In this essay, the popular novelist justifies the existence of horror films.

Reading 6.1

Why We Crave Horror Movies
by Stephen King

1   I think that we're all mentally ill; those of us outside the asylums only hide it a little better—and maybe not all that much better, after all. We've all known people who talk to themselves, people who sometimes squinch their faces into horrible grimaces when they believe no one is watching, people who have some hysterical fear—of snakes, the dark, the tight place, the long drop…and, of course, those final worms and grubs that are waiting so patiently underground.

2   When we pay our four or five bucks, and seat ourselves at tenth-row center in a theater showing a horror movie, we are daring the nightmare.

3   Why? Some of the reasons are simple and obvious. To show that we can, that we are not afraid, that we can ride this roller coaster. Which is not to say that a really good horror movie may not surprise a scream out of us at some point, the way we may scream when the roller coaster twists through a complete 360 or plows through a lake at the bottom of the drop.

And horror movies, like roller coasters, have always been the special province of the young; by the time one turns 40 or 50, one's appetite for double twists or 360-degree loops may be considerably depleted.

4   We also go to re-establish our feelings of essential normality; the horror movie is innately conservative, even reactionary. Freda Jackson as the horrible melting woman in *Die, Monster, Die!* confirms for us that no matter how far we may be removed from the beauty of a Robert Redford or a Diana Ross, we are still light-years from true ugliness.

5   And we go to have fun.

6   Ah, but this is where the ground starts to slope away, isn't it? Because this is a very peculiar sort of fun, indeed. The fun comes from seeing others menaced—sometimes killed. One critic has suggested that if pro football has become the voyeur's version of combat, then the horror film has become the modern version of the public lynching.

7   It is true that the mythic, "fairy-tale" horror film intends to take away the shades of gray....It urges us to put away our more civilized and adult penchant for analysis and to become children again, seeing things in pure blacks and whites. It may be that horror movies provide psychic relief on this level because this invitation to lapse into simplicity, irrationality and even outright madness is extended so rarely. We are told we may allow our emotions a free rein...or no rein at all.

8   If we are all insane, then sanity becomes a matter of degree. If your insanity leads you to carve up women like Jack the Ripper or the Cleveland Torso Murderer, we clap you away in the funny farm (but neither of those two amateur-night surgeons was ever caught, heh-heh-heh); if, on the other hand, your insanity leads you only to talk to yourself when you're under stress or to pick your nose on your morning bus, then you are left alone to go about your business...though it is doubtful that you will ever be invited to the best parties.

9   The potential lyncher is in almost all of us (excluding saints, past and present; but then, most saints have been crazy in their own ways), and every now and then, he has to be let loose to scream and roll around in the grass. Our emotions and our fears form their own body, and we recognize that it demands its own exercise to maintain proper muscle tone. Certain of these emotional muscles are accepted—even exalted—in civilized society; they are, of course, the emotions that tend to maintain the status quo of civilization itself. Love, friendship, loyalty, kindness—these are all the emotions that we applaud, emotions that have been immortalized in the couplets of Hallmark cards and in the verses (I don't dare call it poetry) of Leonard Nimoy.

10   When we exhibit these emotions, society showers us with positive reinforcement; we learn this even before we get out of diapers. When, as children, we hug our rotten little puke of a sister and give her a kiss, all the aunts and uncles smile and twit and cry, "Isn't he the sweetest little thing?" Such coveted treats as chocolate-covered graham crackers often follow. But if we deliberately slam the rotten little puke of a sister's fingers in the door, sanctions follow—angry remonstrance from parents, aunts and uncles; instead of a chocolate-covered graham cracker, a spanking.

11 But anticivilization emotions don't go away, and they demand periodic exercise. We have such "sick" jokes as, "What's the difference between a truckload of bowling balls and a truckload of dead babies?" (You can't unload a truck of bowling balls with a pitchfork...a joke, by the way, that I heard originally from a ten-year-old). Such a joke may surprise a laugh or a grin out of us even as we recoil, a possibility that confirms the thesis: If we share a brotherhood of man, then we also share an insanity of man. None of which is intended as a defense of either the sick joke or insanity but merely as an explanation of why the best horror films, like the best fairy tales, manage to be reactionary, anarchistic, and revolutionary all at the same time.

12 The mythic horror movie, like the sick joke, has a dirty job to do. It deliberately appeals to all that is worst in us. It is morbidity unchained, our most base instincts let free, our nastiest fantasies realized...and it all happens, fittingly enough, in the dark. For those reasons, good liberals often shy away from horror films. For myself, I like to see the most aggressive of them—*Dawn of the Dead*, for instance—as lifting a trap door in the civilized forebrain and throwing a basket of raw meat to the hungry alligators swimming around in that subterranean river beneath.

13 Why bother? Because it keeps them from getting out, man. It keeps them down there and me up here. It was Lennon and McCartney who said that all you need is love, and I would agree with that.

14 As long as you keep the gators fed.

VOCABULARY

Guess the meaning of the words in Column A by matching them with the possible definitions in Column B. Write the letter of the matching definition in the space provided. The number in parentheses indicates the paragraph where the word can be found.

Column A			Column B	
1. *squinch*	(1)	_____	**A.**	to elevate or honor
2. *dare*	(2)	_____	**B.**	to smile broadly
3. *slope*	(6)	_____	**C.**	a mob hanging
4. *lynch*	(6)	_____	**D.**	to embrace
5. *exalted*	(9)	_____	**E.**	a pronged utensil
6. *hug*	(10)	_____	**F.**	to challenge
7. *covet*	(10)	_____	**G.**	to scrunch up facial muscles
8. *grin*	(11)	_____	**H.**	lust after or desire
9. *pitchfork*	(11)	_____	**I.**	to incline

A word may have more than one meaning, depending on how it is used. Find the word in the paragraph (paragraph number is indicated in parentheses) and decide which definition is closest in meaning to the way the word is used in the story. Circle the letter of the appropriate definition.

10. plow (3)   a) a large farming tool that is pulled across soil to turn it over
b) to crash through something
c) the act of turning over soil using a plow

11. clap (8)   a) to put something quickly and firmly away
b) to hit your hands together to express appreciation
c) the loud, sudden noise of thunder

12. Find a two-word expression in paragraph 12 that means "to balk at, or be unwilling to do something." _____

READING COMPREHENSION

1. We go to horror movies to have fun. "But this is a very peculiar sort of fun, indeed." (para. 6) Why is going to horror movies "a peculiar sort of fun"?

_____

2. Why does Stephen King write "heh, heh, heh" in paragraph 8?

_____

What does this tell you about Stephen King's tone, or attitude towards his material?

_____

3. Stephen King concludes his essay with an unusual image. He sees the most aggressive horror films as "lifting a trap door in the civilized forebrain and throwing a basket of raw meat to the hungry alligators swimming around in that subterranean river beneath." What does he mean?

_____

_____

4. Stephen King justifies our need to watch horror movies. In his introduction, he explains that we are all mentally ill, and we need to "dare the nightmare." Find the five reasons that Stephen King gives to explain "why we crave horror movies," and find one fact or example from the text to support each reason.

a) _____

(Support) _____

b) _____

(Support) _____

c) _____

(Support) _____

d) _____

(Support) _____

e) _____

(Support) _____

DISCUSSION

1. Stephen King, in his introduction, states that we're all mentally ill. Is this an effective way to introduce his essay? Why or why not? Do you agree that we're all mentally ill?

2. We do crazy, adventurous things "to show that we are not afraid." What sorts of dangerous things have you or your friends done? Why do you take crazy chances?

3. "The potential lyncher is in almost all of us." Do you agree with this statement? Why or why not?

4. Stephen King says that horror movies "are conservative, even reactionary," (para. 4) but he does not elaborate on this point. How are horror movies conservative?

5. What are some of the horror movies that you've seen? Are there different types of horror movies? Are some horror movies more "harmless" than others?

Writing Tips

The Introduction

In Stephen King's essay, he effectively gets our attention by making the outrageous statement: "We're all mentally ill." At the same time, he makes us think about what he is saying, and he piques our interest so that we continue reading.

Introductions should arouse the reader's interest in the topic. Making a controversial statement, as Stephen King did, is one way to get the reader's attention. However, there are many other ways to stimulate the reader's interest, and at the same time draw the reader into your argument.

Introduction Styles

Imagine that you were asked to write an essay on the following topic: "Cats are better pets than dogs."

You could begin with:

1. Anecdote   Tell a brief anecdote that relates, in some way, to your topic.

> One day, when I was really feeling alone, I sat on my couch to mope. Suddenly I felt little paws on my lap…

2. Description   Describe something related to your topic.

> Green, almond–shaped eyes stare at me. The fur gleams, …

3. Historical Background Information   Begin an essay by discussing the history of your topic.

> In ancient Egypt, cats were considered sacred, and many monuments to the cat were constructed…

An introduction must also present the thesis, or main point, of the essay.

Avoid the following Introduction Problems:

1. I'm going to talk about…
This is obvious. DO NOT begin an essay this way.

2. Cats are better pets than dogs because they are cleaner, more independent and more cuddly.
Avoid giving away all of your arguments in the introduction. Simply state your point of view in an interesting way, and save your supporting arguments for the body of your essay. (Note: Some writing manuals disagree with this point. If your teacher wants you to present your main arguments in the introduction, then you should do it.)

WRITING TIPS EXERCISE 1

Read the following introductions and then answer the questions below.

A	B
Violence in the media does not turn impressionable children into killers. When I was a child, I grew up on a diet of the *Power Rangers*, and I played with toy guns. My brother and I alternately blasted each other with the toys and then had elaborate death scenes. "You've hit me again," I would cry, clutching my stomach and rolling over. My body would jerk a few times and then lie still. Within seconds of the "death" I would run and hide behind the couch, shoot my brother, and he would act out a similar scene. My brother and I watched violent television shows and we played with toy guns, yet now, as adults, we are both peace-loving pacifists.	Since the early days of cinema, audiences have been entertained with scary films. The first audiences to see *King Kong* fainted from fear. Later, *Frankenstein* and *Dracula* terrorized the population. Early directors managed to create suspenseful, horrifying movies without showing the gory details. Alfred Hitchcock didn't have to show us the "birds" picking out people's eyes to incite terror in his audiences. Yet today's directors leave nothing to the imagination. In *Pulp Fiction*, every violent moment is explored in all its gory, disgusting detail. Extremely violent images are unnecessary, and there should be limits to the amount of violence in films.

1. Find the thesis statement in Introduction A and highlight it. Look again at the list of introduction styles. Introduction A is an example of which style? _____

2. Find the thesis statement in Introduction B and highlight it. Introduction B is an example of which style? _____

WRITING TIPS EXERCISE 2

Read the following essay, "The Disadvantages of Being a Teen Parent." Underline the topic sentences in each paragraph. Then, on a separate piece of paper, write three different introductions for this essay, using one of the following devices for each introduction:

    a) historical background

    b) an anecdote

    c) a description

The Disadvantages of Being a Teen Parent

(Write three introductions.)

When a teenager becomes a parent, there are a multitude of responsibilities that come with the baby. The baby must be fed, cleaned, entertained and cared for day and night. Babies do not stop crying just because daddy is tired of listening to them, and they do not stop asking for attention just because mommy has had a long, hard day.

In addition to the extra responsibilities, perhaps the most unpleasant aspect of being a teen parent is that the teenager can no longer do the things that his or her friends are doing. Experiences such as going to university, traveling and finding romance become almost impossible when the expense and demands of the child are considered. When friends go off to Europe for a holiday, or plan a trip across Canada during the summer, the teenage parent must stay behind. Even just going to a movie, a party or for a coffee with friends becomes difficult when a baby's needs are factored in.

Before every outing, the teen parent has to decide who will watch the baby. How will the baby-sitter be paid? The dollar spent on a coffee easily becomes a $20 outing when baby-sitting fees are factored in. With so many extra expenses, the teenage parent's need for extra money becomes acute, and the difficulty of getting that extra money is compounded by the presence of the baby. Babies cannot be brought to work. Daycare fees in Canada range from $400 to $1000 per month, depending on the province, so teenage parents have a difficult time earning enough simply to cover daycare expenses.

The decision to have a baby means that the teenager's life changes, forever. The teen parent must make huge economic and social sacrifices. If you are a teenager, and the idea of having your own cute baby in your arms appeals to you, babysit someone else's child for a week. And remember, the cute little baby does not stay cute, or little, for long.

Writing Suggestion

Write an essay with an introduction, two or three supporting paragraphs and a conclusion. Before you begin writing, make an essay plan. Choose one of the following topics:

1. What are horror movies?
2. Horror movies are conservative.
3. The best horror movie is ...
4. We are all insane.
5. The potential lyncher is in all of us.

1. In groups, exchange stories about dangerous things you or your friends have done. Try to explain why you do such dangerous things. Why do you think younger people take more chances than older people?

2. Divide the class into teams of six. Then each team must be broken into three groups with two students each. Each group of two must write an introduction for the topic: "The Best Horror Movie." In each team:

a) one pair write an "anecdote" introduction.

b) one pair write a "descriptive" introduction.

c) one pair write a "background information" introduction.

These introductions are not to be handed in, so the students can simply jot down their main points. After 15 minutes, the teams must present their introductions to the class orally. Students can vote on which team wrote the most effective introduction of each style.

Shame

The following essay was written by a well-known satirist. In the 1960s and 1970s, Dick Gregory was a stand-up comedian and he appeared on various television shows. Gregory has been active in the civil rights movement in the United States.

In the following essay from his 1964 autobiography, *Nigger*, Gregory describes a childhood experience that taught him the meaning of shame.

Reading 7.1
Shame
by Dick Gregory

1   I never learned hate at home, or shame. I had to go to school for that. I was about seven years old when I got my first big lesson. I was in love with a girl named Helene Tucker, a light-complexioned little girl with pigtails and nice manners. She was always clean and she was smart in school. In think I went to school then mostly to look at her. I brushed my hair and even got me a little old handkerchief. It was a lady's handkerchief, but I didn't want Helene to see me wipe my nose on my hand. The pipes were frozen again, there was no water in the house, but I washed my socks and shirt every night. I'd get a pot, and go over to Mister Ben's grocery store, and stick my pot down into his soda machine. Scoop out some chopped ice. By evening the ice melted to water for washing. I got sick a lot that winter because the fire would go out at night before the clothes were dry. In the morning I'd put them on, wet or dry, because they were the only clothes I had.

2   Everybody's got a Helene Tucker, a symbol of everything you want. I loved her for her goodness, her cleanness, her popularity. She'd walk down my street and my brothers and sisters would yell, "Here comes Helene," and I'd rub my tennis sneakers on the back of my pants and wish my hair wasn't so nappy and the white folks' shirt fit me better. I'd run out on the street. If I knew my place and didn't come too close, she'd wink at me and say hello. That was a good feeling. Sometimes I'd follow her all the way home, and shovel the snow off her walk and try to make friends with her Momma and her aunts. I'd drop money on her stoop late at night on my way back from shining shoes in the taverns. And she had a Daddy, and he had a good job. He was a paper hanger.

3   I guess I would have gotten over Helene by summertime, but something happened in that classroom that made her face hang in front of me for the next twenty-two years. When I played the drums in high school it was for Helene and when I broke track records in college it was for Helene and when I started standing behind microphones and heard applause I wished Helene could hear it, too. It wasn't until I was twenty-nine years old and married and making money that I finally got her out of my system. Helene was sitting in that classroom when I learned to be ashamed of myself.

4   It was on a Thursday. I was sitting in the back of the room, in a seat with a chalk circle drawn around it. The idiot's seat, the troublemaker's seat.

5   The teacher thought I was stupid. Couldn't spell, couldn't read, couldn't do arithmetic. Just stupid. Teachers were never interested in finding out that you couldn't concentrate because you were so hungry, because you hadn't had any breakfast. All you could think about was noontime, would it ever come? Maybe you could sneak into the cloakroom and steal a bite of some kid's lunch out of a coat pocket. A bite of something. Paste. You can't really make a meal of paste, or put it on bread for a sandwich, but sometimes I'd scoop a few spoonfuls out of the paste jar in the back of the room. Pregnant people get strange tastes. I was pregnant with poverty. Pregnant with dirt and pregnant with smells that made people turn away, pregnant with cold and pregnant with shoes that were never bought for me, pregnant with five other people in my bed and no Daddy in the next room, and pregnant with hunger. Paste doesn't taste too bad when you're hungry.

6   The teacher thought I was a troublemaker. All she saw from the front of the room was a little black boy who squirmed in his idiot's seat and made noises and poked the kids around him. I guess she couldn't see a kid who made noises because he wanted someone to know he was there.

7   It was on a Thursday, the day before the Negro payday. The eagle always flew on Friday. The teacher was asking each student how much his father would give to the Community Chest. On Friday night, each kid would get the money from his father, and on Monday he would bring it to the school. I decided I was going to buy me a Daddy right then. I had money in my pocket from shining shoes and selling papers, and whatever Helene Tucker pledged for her Daddy I was going to top it. And I'd hand the money right in. I wasn't going to wait until Monday to buy me a Daddy.

8   I was shaking, scared to death. The teacher opened her book and started calling out names alphabetically.

9   "Helene Tucker?"

10   "My daddy said he'd give two dollars and fifty cents."

11   "That's very nice, Helene. Very, very nice indeed."

12   That made me feel pretty good. It wouldn't take too much to top that. I had almost three dollars in dimes and quarters in my pocket. I stuck my hand in my pocket and held onto the money, waiting for her to call my name. But the teacher closed her book after she called everybody else in the class.

13   I stood up and raised my hand.

14   "What is it now?"

15   "You forgot me."

16   She turned toward the blackboard. "I don't have time to be playing with you, Richard."

17   "My Daddy said he'd…"

18   "Sit down, Richard, you're disturbing the class."

19   "My Daddy said he'd give…fifteen dollars."

20   She turned around and looked mad. "We are collecting this money for you and your kind, Richard Gregory. If your Daddy can give fifteen dollars you have no business being on relief."

21   "I got it right now, I got it right now, my Daddy gave it to me to turn in today, my Daddy said…"

22   "And furthermore," she said, looking right at me, her nostrils getting big and her lips getting thin and her eyes opening wide, "we know you don't have a Daddy."

23   Helene Tucker turned around, her eyes full of tears. She felt sorry for me. Then I couldn't see her too well because I was crying, too.

24   "Sit down, Richard."

25   And I always thought the teacher kind of liked me. She always picked me to wash the blackboard on Friday, after school. That was a big thrill, it made me feel important. If I didn't wash it, come Monday the school might not function right.

26   "Where are you going, Richard?"

27   I walked out of school that day, and for a long time I didn't go back very often. There was shame there.

28   Now there was shame everywhere. It seemed like the whole world had been inside that classroom, everyone had heard what the teacher had said, everyone had turned around and felt sorry for me. There was shame in going to the Worthy Boys Annual Christmas Dinner for you and your kind, because everybody knew what a worthy boy was. Why couldn't they just call it the Boys Annual Dinner; why'd they have to give it a name? There was shame in wearing the brown and orange and white plaid mackinaw the welfare gave to three thousand boys. Why'd it have to be the same for everybody so when you walked down the street the people could see you were on relief? It was a nice warm mackinaw and it had a hood, and my Momma beat me and called me a little rat when she found out I stuffed it in the bottom of a pail full of garbage way over on Cottage Street. There was shame in running over to Mister Ben's at the end of the day and asking for his rotten peaches, there was shame in asking Mrs. Simmons for a spoonful of sugar, there was shame in running out to meet the relief truck. I hated that truck, full of food for you and your kind. I ran into the house and hid when it came. And then I started to sneak through alleys, to take the long way home so the people going into White's Eat Shop wouldn't see me. Yeah, the whole world heard the teacher that day, we all know you don't have a Daddy.

VOCABULARY

Match the verbs in Column A with their definitions in Column B. Write the letter of the matching definition in the space provided. The numbers in parentheses indicate the paragraph where the verb can be found.

Column A			Column B	
1. *wipe*	(1)	_____	**A.**	to dig out something using a spade-like tool
2. *wink*	(2)	_____	**B.**	to go stealthily or slyly
3. *shovel*	(2)	_____	**C.**	to lift out a handful
4. *sneak*	(5)	_____	**D.**	to dry by rubbing
5. *scoop*	(5)	_____	**E.**	to close and open one eye quickly
6. *squirm*	(6)	_____	**F.**	to be unable to stay still; to twist about

7. Circle the letter for the definition of the word *pledge* as it is used in paragraph 7.
    a) to drink to the health of someone
    b) a gift promised to charity
    c) the state of being held in security

8. What is a "worthy boy"? (para. 28)

_____

READING COMPREHENSION

1. What is the thesis statement in Dick Gregory's introduction?

_____

2. Gregory says, "Everybody's got a Helene Tucker, a symbol of everything you want." (para. 2) Why was Helene a symbol for him?

_____

3. What are some of the things that Gregory did to impress Helene?

_____

_____

4. Why was Gregory a "troublemaker" at school?

_____

_____

5. Why did the teacher neglect to call on Gregory when she was collecting for the community chest?

_____

6. Why did Helene's face "hang in front of" Gregory for 22 years?

DISCUSSION

1. What could the teacher have done, when collecting money, so as not to embarrass Gregory?

2. How do you think Dick Gregory finally got Helene out of his system?

3. According to Canadian writer Elizabeth Smart, "pain burns a hole through time." Would you agree with this? Do you have sharper memories of painful moments than of happy ones?

4. Gregory's essay tells a story. Does it teach us anything, as well?

5. Because Gregory was both poor and black, he felt doubly left out of mainstream society. In your opinion, is it possible for a completely prejudice-free society to exist? Do you think that any country, city or village on the planet contains a completely non-racist population?

 *riting Tips*

The Conclusion

A good conclusion should bring an essay to a satisfactory close.

To write an effective conclusion:

1. restate the thesis, or main point, of the essay.

2. briefly restate, but do not repeat, the main arguments that you used to support your opinion.

3. end the essay with a suggestion, a prediction, a solution or an interesting quote. Your essay should end by giving the readers something to think about.

 ## WRITING TIPS EXERCISE

Read the following opinion essay. Highlight the thesis statement as well as the topic sentences in each paragraph, and then write an effective conclusion.

Actors for Hire

I work in a restaurant. I take orders from cranky customers, I carry heavy trays filled with food, and I stay on my feet for ten-hour shifts. I get blisters on my toes, and back aches. At the end of the day, including tips, I average about $8 per hour. If I want to relax and watch a movie at the cinema, I must pay more than I earn per hour for the privilege of seeing some spoiled actors do their wooden acting in often ridiculous movies. Sylvester Stallone earns more than some small nations for his roles in violent, forgettable flicks. Actors are grossly overpaid, and the movie industry should put a stop to it!

First of all, it is becoming exceedingly difficult for most of us working stiffs to go to a film because of the steep ticket and concession stand prices. Movies cost over $8, and that is before you calculate the cost of popcorn! You all know that the drinks are over $2 each, and the small popcorn is over $3. For a couple to see a movie, it costs almost $30 for the evening. If film studios earn enough to pay Jim Carrey $20 million, then some of the profits could be taken off the actors' salaries and the ticket prices could be reduced.

Demi Moore earned $12 million for her role as a stripper. Company presidents earn considerably less. Teachers, doctors, social workers, nurses and fire fighters probably wouldn't even accept such a ridiculous salary, because NOBODY needs that type of money! You can support a family on $50 thousand per year. You can have a swimming pool and a big house, and take frequent trips for $.5 million per year. The entire staff of a local manufacturing company earned less last year than Jim Carrey earned in three months!

With their huge salaries, movie actors live decadent lives in a time when most people in North America are struggling to make ends meet. A slouching New York actor has a limo follow him on his walks through town in case he gets tired. A famous actress bought a Victorian mansion just to have a place to keep her huge doll collection! A well known young actor buys new clothing in every city he visits rather than bother with luggage. The overly large salaries just turn these actors into spoiled brats.

(Write a conclusion.)

Writing Suggestion

Choose one of the following topics, and write an opinion essay. Remember to write an essay plan and to write an effective introduction and conclusion.

1. Pain burns a hole through time.
2. It is possible (or impossible) to have a prejudice-free society.
3. People are prejudiced because...

Speaking Suggestion

Students should get into groups. Each group could have a discussion about prejudice. What are examples of prejudice attitudes in our community? What are the causes of these prejudiced attitudes? What are some possible solutions for the problem?

Each group should choose its best solution and present it to the rest of the class.

Mission Improbable

Reading 8.1

Mission Improbable
by Susan Reed and Cathy Nolan

Most of us have marveled at the performances of elephants in circuses and been awed by their size and power. Yet how much do we really know about these creatures? In the following article, Susan Reed and Cathy Nolan examine the remarkable work of Daphne Sheldrick. Established in Nairobi, Sheldrick operates an orphanage for elephants.

1   Last October, a land cruiser truck carrying the limp body of a month-old African elephant pulled up to the gate of Daphne Sheldrick's property just outside of Kenya's Nairobi National Park. It had been found wandering alone outside another park dazed and dehydrated, its floppy ears badly sunburned. "The babies are always ill and sometimes severely traumatized," says Sheldrick now as she tends the new arrival, applying antiseptic powder to its ears and to a wound on its leg. "Constant affection, attention, touching and communication are crucial to their will to live. They must never be left alone."

2   Remarkably, those that make it to the Sheldrick homestead never are. Until they are 2, they get all the attention that a human infant would receive—including having a keeper sleep at their side every night. Sheldrick, 61, the widow of David Sheldrick, a renowned naturalist and founder of Kenya's Tsavo National Park, opened her elephant and rhino orphanage in 1977 and has become a leading authority on infant elephant behavior. After 25 years of frustrating trial and error, she developed a system for nurturing baby elephants. Her method includes a skim milk-coconut oil formula devised for human babies—young pachyderms

cannot digest the fat in cow's milk—a small amount of elephant dung to provide digestion-enhancing bacteria and round-the-clock human contact. In 1987 she became the first person to hand-raise a wild, milk-dependent baby elephant. Since then, she and her staff of eight keepers have raised 12 elephants from infancy—the highest success rate in the world. "What Daphne gives them is hands-on care," says Tony Fitzjohn, a Kenyan conservationist. "It's what they need, and it's extremely hard work."

3   Especially when elephants arrive damaged. The newest, which Sheldrick has named Sungelai (Swahili for "mighty warrior"), consumes about 10 quarts of formula—plus eight quarts of additional fluid and salts—to help him rehydrate. He receives his bottles through a hole in a gray blanket hung between two trees, which replicates the shape and feel of a mother elephant's belly. Sheldrick's keepers rotate 6-hour shifts, playing with him, taking him on walks—and occasionally disciplining him.

4   "Infant elephants are very similar to human infants," says Sheldrick. "They can be naughty, competitive and disobedient: When you say, 'No,' they want to do it." If punishment is called for, Sheldrick gives them "a little zing on the bum" with a battery-powered cattle prod. "It's an unfamiliar sensation, so it's unpleasant for them. But then," she adds, "you have to be careful to make friends with them again." Prodigious memory may explain why zookeepers are occasionally killed by elephants they have known for years. "They've done something to the elephant which they've forgotten, but the elephant hasn't," Sheldrick explains.

5   For every step forward, there were painful retreats. In 1974, while at Tsavo, Sheldrick achieved a breakthrough when she nursed a newborn, Aisha, to 6 months. But then she had to leave for two weeks to attend her daughter Jill's wedding. Aisha, who had bonded exclusively with Sheldrick—stopped eating. "She died of a broken heart," says Sheldrick, who now rotates keepers to prevent babies from bonding with only one person.

6   The orphans remain at Sheldrick's Nairobi compound until the age of 2, when they are fully weaned onto a vegetable diet. Once they are able to feed themselves, they are trucked to Tsavo National Park, 150 miles away, where they are put into a stockade and gradually introduced to local herds. Eleanor, 38, who was rescued by Sheldrick's first husband and reintroduced into the wild in 1970, has become a willing adoptive mother. "The little elephants are always welcome in a wild herd," says Sheldrick.

7   But the adults can also be stern parents. "If the matriarch gives them a smack with her truck, they'll come flying back to their human keepers," says Sheldrick, who makes sure the youngsters are free to come and go from the stockade. "It takes 12 to 15 years [of their 60- to 70-year lifespan] before the baby becomes independent of his human family. Eventually they get bored stiff with people because they're having more fun with elephants."

8   For their part, elephants can make it instantly clear when humans have overstepped their welcome. Last year, Sheldrick was visiting Tsavo when mistakenly she thought she had spotted Eleanor. "I called to her, and she came over," she recalls. "I talked to her for about 10 minutes and touched her ear. She didn't like that at all and used her tusk and trunk to send me flying into a pile of boulders." Despite a shattered right knee and femur from which she is

still recovering, Sheldrick doesn't hold a grudge. "On the contrary," she says, "I'm very flattered that a completely wild elephant would come talk to me."

9   Sheldrick's affinity for animals showed up early in life. The third of four children born to farmers Brian and Marjorie Jenkins, she grew up near Kenya's Rift Valley and took care of her first orphan, a duiker antelope, when she was 3. She was still a teen in 1953 when she married game warden Bill Woodley and moved to Tsavo National Part, where their daughter Jill, now 40, was born. The marriage failed because of Woodley's long absences, and they were divorced in 1959. The following year she married David Sheldrick, Tsavo's founding warden—and Woodley's boss—with whom she had a daughter, Angela, 32.

10   For the next 16 years, Sheldrick lived a life straight out of *Born Free*, learning the behavior of native animals from orphans—including wild rhino, buffalo, zebra, impala, eland, reedbuck, warthog, mongoose, antelope and birds brought to her by park rangers. "When you raise an orphan, you need to know how that animal lives in the wild, whether it's gregarious and needs a family or solitary and needs seclusion," she says. "You have to duplicate natural conditions. And you have to take care of its mind as well as its body. Each elephant," says Sheldrick, "has his own story. Kika grieved for months for his family that was killed by poachers. Emily had endless stomach problems. Aitong arrived with pneumonia and a head injury that made her walk in circles."

11   In 1976, David Sheldrick was transferred to Nairobi but the next year suddenly died of a heart attack. Daphne received permission from the government to build a three-bedroom bungalow at the edge of Nairobi National Park, 15 miles outside the capital. In 1977 she established her orphanage—and began to form the David Sheldrick Wildlife Trust to fund her work. Her efforts have earned her a Member of the Order of the British Empire and election to the United Nations Environment Program Global 500 list of achievers.

12   The pace of adoptions has ebbed since the sale of ivory was banned internationally in 1989 (in the '70s and '80s poachers slaughtered more than 150,000 of Kenya's elephants for their tusks), leaving Sheldrick more time to write and lecture. Still, baby elephants continue to be separated from their herds accidentally. And Sheldrick wants every one of them to have a foster family.

13   Hers. On a recent afternoon, she looked on maternally as Sungelai mischievously butted one of his keepers. "He was demoralized and cross when he came in," she says. "Since then, his tummy has stabilized and he's put on 100 pounds. You can tell he's quite a pushy little guy," she adds with pride. "And he's started playing. That's always a very good sign."

VOCABULARY

1. An African elephant was found "wandering alone outside another park dazed and dehydrated, its floppy ears badly sunburned." Define the following:

a) *wandering* _____

b) *dazed* _____

c) *floppy* _____

2. Find another word for *elephant* in paragraph 2. _____

3. What is a *cattle prod* and what does Sheldrick use it for? (para. 4)

_____

_____

_____

4. Define *prodigious*. (para. 4)

_____

_____

READING COMPREHENSION

1. What technique does the writer use in the introduction? (description, narration or background information)

_____

2. What types of support (both physical and emotional) do baby elephants need?

_____

_____

_____

3. Why did the newborn elephant, Aisha, die?

_____

_____

4. How successful has Sheldrick been at reintroducing elephants into the wild?

_____

_____

5. Generally, how long does it take for an elephant to become independent in the wild, after being raised by humans?

_____

6. What is the writer's purpose, or goal, with this story?

_____

_____

DISCUSSION

1. What are emotions? Some people claim that only humans feel emotions. Is there any evidence in the text to refute this notion? What is the evidence? Have you heard about any other types of animals that may feel emotions?

2. Have you ever seen an elephant in a circus? In a zoo? Do you think that it is OK to keep elephants in captivity? Should all zoos and aquariums be closed down? Why or why not?

3. This article focuses on some endearing qualities in baby elephants. Undoubtedly many other mammals also have endearing qualities, yet many of us do the following: we eat cattle; we kill minks, seals and foxes for their fur; we wear leather and buckskin. Some of us even hunt animals for pleasure. Ask yourself the following questions:
   a) Is there ever a good reason to kill a mammal?
   b) Should we distinguish between warm- and cold-blooded creatures?
   c) Why would most people accept the killing of a snake, but not the killing of a baby seal?
   d) What about birds, fish or insects? Where do we draw the line?

4. Animals are used in the testing of cosmetics, and to test new medical inventions. Should animals be used for these purposes? Is testing on animals unethical? Is it necessary? Are some types of experiments on animals valid, whereas others are not?

Writing Tips

Transitions between Paragraphs

If you were to ride on a train, and pieces of the track were missing, you would be in for a very bumpy ride. When you write an essay, there must be transitional phrases between paragraphs to ensure that the reader has a smooth ride through your arguments.

In order to guide the reader from one idea to the next, or from one paragraph to the next, there are some methods that can be employed.

1. Briefly refer to the previous argument, and link it to your current argument. For example, in a text about the superiority of cats, the paragraphs could contain the following points:

Paragraph 1 subject: *Cats are more independent than dogs*

Paragraph 2 subject: *Cats are cleaner than dogs*

Topic sentence for second body paragraph — with transition:

Not only does a cat happily stay home alone, but it keeps itself neatly groomed while you are away.

In this sentence the reader is briefly reminded of the previous point (the independence of cats) and then introduced to the next point (the neatness of cats).

2. With a transitional word or phrase, lead the reader to your next idea.

Furthermore, the cat, unlike the dog, keeps itself neatly groomed.

Transitional Words and Phrases

Chronology (adding ideas)	Contrasting Ideas	Adding Emphasis	Examples
first, second, third	on the other hand	in fact	for example
furthermore	whereas	certainly	such as
moreover	nevertheless	undoubtedly	for instance
in addition	and yet	surely	to illustrate
also	although	beyond a doubt	
besides	on the contrary	definitely	
then	in spite of (despite)		
finally	however		

Concluding

in conclusion	to conclude
to sum up	consequently
therefore (thus)	in short

WRITING TIPS EXERCISE

Write topic sentences for each paragraph, and make sure that you use transitional words or phrases. The first paragraph (the introduction) does not require any changes.

Canadian cities have rushed into the casino market, and cities in almost every Canadian province now contain sparkling new casinos. Even Regina, Saskatchewan, recently opened one. Government-run casinos are great for society, or disastrous for society, depending on the person that you speak to. The question is, who should we believe?

(Body 1)

_____

_____

Tourists visit the area and deposit money directly into the local economy. Restaurants and hotels benefit from the influx of tourist dollars. Even when locals use the casino, the money they spend is like a voluntary tax. If people want to give away their cash, it's not the government's responsibility to stop them.

(Body 2)

_____

_____

The majority of customers in most casino cities are local customers. This means that local gambling addicts are given an ideal scenario to gamble away their life-savings. Gambling-related suicides occur, and some families are reduced to visiting food banks after monthly paychecks are gambled away.

(Conclusion)

_____

_____

Obviously, if a government spokesperson discusses this issue, he or she is not going to dwell on the negative impact of casinos. Groups helping the gambling addicted can paint a portrait of a local menace. The truth about the issue is probably to be found somewhere in between these two polar views.

Writing Suggestion

Write an essay with an introduction, two or three supporting paragraphs, and a conclusion. Use transitional words and phrases when necessary. You can choose one of the following topics:

1. Should elephants ever be kept in captivity?
2. My pet shows emotional reactions.
3. Experiments using animals should (or should not) be banned.
4. Wild animals should not be put on public display.

Speaking Suggestion

Choose one of the topics listed in Writing Suggestions. In small groups, debate the given issue. When your group has come to a consensus, share your views with other class members.

Research Topics

The essays in this chapter look at controversial issues. You will be required to use the essays as launching pads for a researched essay. It is important that you look in the library, on the Internet or in magazines and newspapers for other views about the subject that you choose.

Reading 9.1 ## Bad News About the Effects of Divorce
by Lloyd Billingsley

In the past twenty years, the divorce rate has sky-rocketed. The royal family in Britain has captivated the public's attention with the divorces of three out of four of the royal offspring. Divorce, banned by the Catholic church, and frowned upon historically, has become as common as the running shoe.

The current generation of youths are the first, perhaps in modern history, to live in a society where families easily break up, and varieties of new mixed families are created. Are children better off if their unhappy parents divorce? Lloyd Billingsley examines the effects of divorce on children in the following article.

1   The most extensive study of divorced families ever undertaken has yielded grave findings and has seriously challenged the conventional wisdom on the subject.

2   The Children of Divorce project, begun in northern California in 1971, studied 60 divorced families spanning a variety of racial and economic backgrounds. The 131 children involved ranged from 3–18 years of age.

3   Judith Wallerstein, founder of the project, is a psychologist at the University of California at Berkeley and also operates the Center for the Family in Transition in nearby Corte Madera. Her interest in the effects of divorce on children began when she moved to California after 17 years at the Menninger Foundation. When schools and social agencies asked questions about children and divorce, she found no adequate research on the subject and began her own. One

of her goals was to test the "dogma" that a divorce that allegedly promotes the happiness of the adults is also good for the children, something she calls a "typically adult argument." She interviewed all members of the 60 families at various stages during the study. Originally, she expected the project to last only one year, after which time she assumed that most of the damaging effects of divorce, like those of bereavement, would have abated. Such did not prove to be the case. She found the damage to be acute still—10 years after the study started.

4   Many of the children—37 percent—were found to be "consciously and intensely unhappy and dissatisfied with their life in the post-divorce family." Many of them were "intensely lonely" and complained of coming home after school to an empty house. Divorced parents' readjustment to single life often made them feel left out. Even in remarried families, children felt abandoned or shunned by the newly married couple, whose main concern often seemed to be privacy.

5   Strong anger—especially directed at the father—remained years after the marriage breakup. Older boys and adolescents were among those most likely to exhibit outbursts of temper or violent behavior. Others refused contact with fathers, even returning their birthday gifts to them unopened.

6   Wallerstein expected that children who had been rejected would feel powerless and troubled, but she was unprepared for the depths of misery in some of them. One nine-year-old, reminded of his policeman father by the sound of a siren, launched into a 35-minute crying spell in the presence of interviewers.

7   Twenty-nine percent of the 131 children represented a middle ground of psychological health between those described as "depressed" and those who were "coping." This group showed average academic and social progress, but Wallerstein noted "islands of unhappiness" in them that did not bode well for future development.

8   Thirty-four percent of the children, a group representing both sexes and all ages, were found to be psychologically resilient and coping well with their changed life. However, even among this group, many of them still felt lonely, unhappy, or sorrowful about what had happened. They harbored vivid, detailed memories of the breakup even after 10 years.

9   In almost all cases, the first news of the divorce came as a shock, with the children neither seeing it as a solution to their problems nor experiencing feelings of relief. They considered their situation to be no worse than that of anyone else and would have been content to carry on. The divorce, Wallerstein says, was "a bolt of lightning that struck them when they had not even been aware of a need to come in from the storm."

10   The faithfulness of the children to their original families surprised the researchers and proved unsettling to some of the parents. Many children clung to fantasies of a magical connection between their parents; still others replied "which one?" to questions about their fathers years after the divorce.

11   Fatherly visits did help to diminish dependency on one parent, but Wallerstein describes these relationships as "offering the children little in fully addressing the complex tasks of growing up." Neither new friends nor grandparents, although helpful, were found able to fill the voids in the children's lives.

12   Brother-sister relationships among children from divorced families continued to be strong. The enduring ties Wallerstein describes as almost constituting a kind of "sub–family."

13   The older children of divorce showed a surprisingly strong commitment to the concept of the family and definitely did not want to wind up divorced themselves. In many cases, they wanted to delay both marriage (often desiring to live together first) and having children.

14   Concerning the causes of divorce, Wallerstein believes that in most cases, "there was never really a marriage." Where true intimacy and oneness were lacking, the marriage was unable to bear the stresses of life—children, deaths in the family, change, and economic woes. Wallerstein acknowledges that many people have been "carried away" in equating eroticism with happiness in recent years. A number of husbands in the project had been having extramarital affairs.

15   In spite of finding it "clear" that the divorced family is, "in many ways less adaptive economically, socially, and psychologically to the raising of children than the two-parent family," Wallerstein believes that divorce should remain "a readily available option." But impulsive, frivolous divorce she views as disastrous, especially in cases where the couple has been married for many years. She values highly the institution of marriage and supports all efforts (such as Marriage Encounter and similar projects) to strengthen the marriage bond.

16   With the millions who are already victims of divorce, she has encouraged clergy and church groups to become involved. "Divorce is like no other stress," she says, pointing out that the emotional support that is quickly forthcoming in cases such as death is absent in a divorce; relatives tend toward aloofness or abandonment. The church, she avers, should marshal its resources to "fight loneliness." Those who would be effective therapists and comforters she counsels to acquire training with children.

17   Wallerstein and her associates are currently planning a study of children from nondivorced families, intending to compare the results with the Children of Divorce project.

VOCABULARY

1. Find a word in paragraph 3 that means "an anguished emotional state caused by the death of a close loved one."

_____

2. "Children felt abandoned or shunned by the newly married couple." (para. 4) What is the meaning of *shunned?*

_____

3. Find a phrase in paragraph 7 that means "it was not a good sign."

_____

4. Find a two-word expression in paragraph 13 that means "to finish or end up."

_____

5. Find a word in paragraph 15 that means "foolish, not serious."

_____

READING COMPREHENSION

1. A study of divorced families began in what year?

_____

2. How extensive was the study? How many people were studied, and what types of people were studied?

_____

_____

3. Do most children know that their family is about to break up? Explain your answer.

_____

_____

_____

4. Lloyd Billingsley concludes that divorce is bad for children. What proof does he offer for this view?

_____

_____

_____

_____

_____

5. According to the article, what are some of the causes of divorce?

_____

_____

_____

DISCUSSION

1. Billingsley wrote this article in 1982. Since then divorce has become more acceptable in our society. Are the findings in the article outdated? Explain your answer.

2. What can be done to lower the divorce rate? Should it be more difficult for people to divorce? Should it be more difficult for people to marry?

3. What are the most difficult things for a child to adjust to when his or her parents divorce?

4. What can divorced parents do to make the divorce as painless as possible for the children?

5. Can divorce be good for the children? In what circumstances? Do you believe that divorce traumatizes some children for life?

6. Do you believe that it is possible to love the same person, and be happily married for a lifetime? How could this be achieved?

Reading 9.2

The Starvation Demons
by Adrienne Webb

Great numbers of North American citizens are walking advertisements. We advertise sports teams on our caps and local clubs on our T-shirts. Our sneakers contain bold letters or symbols that advertise a particular shoe company, such as Nike. Our jeans have labels that prominently display the jeans company. Some people even let their underwear show in order to display the Calvin Klein logo.

We can't really get away from advertising. Everywhere we go we see ads: on billboards, on the sides of buses and at bus stops, in store windows, on the TV, in print journalism and so on. Could this advertising actually be harming us? The following essay presents the relationship between advertising and harmful, self-destructive behavior.

1   She sprawls on the couch, talking about this and that—her classes in psychology, a recent writing assignment for a local alternative newspaper—but Jenna is unlike most 20-year-olds contemplating their lives. For her, life itself—not the academic career she has been compelled to set aside—has become the challenge because she has a debilitating, and potentially deadly, ailment. Last December, Jenna, who requested anonymity, felt suicidal and went to Vancouver's St. Paul's Hospital. At five feet, four inches, she weighed 90 pounds—but was convinced she had eaten too much. She was diagnosed as having anorexia nervosa, a

disorder in which young people, mostly women, starve themselves. Jenna now realizes that she wasn't overeating, but she still wrestles with her demons. "I just don't want to eat," says Jenna. "My big concern is that I spent three years trying to lose weight, and by eating I'm going to put it all back on in a month."

2   Anorexia nervosa is a tough opponent. It is characterized not only by extreme weight loss and a morbid fear of becoming fat—regardless of weight—but by low self-esteem, distorted body image and a failure to recognize how serious the condition is. Anorexics typically weigh less than 85 percent of the normal minimum for their age and height and 95 percent of them are female. Eating disorders are not an affliction of middle-class women chasing physical perfection. Says Peggy Claude-Pierre, program director at Montreux Counselling Centre in Victoria: "This is not about vanity."

3   But it may, in part, be a reaction to the manic body-worshippers of commercial television and the fitness and travel industries. Vicki Smye, a clinical nurse specialist at the St. Paul's clinic, says people with eating disorders often have low self-esteem and find it difficult to be assertive. And while anorexia nervosa is not strictly about body image, the unrealistic goals put forward by popular culture can become an unfortunate focus for already troubled people. As an indication of how pervasive the imagery of Western culture can be, Smye says, eating disorders have even begun to emerge in societies where they were once uncommon, such as Japan.

4   There is support for that indictment of cultural hype. Dr. Paul Garfinkel of Toronto's Clarke Institute of Psychiatry, an expert in eating disorders, says the illnesses are magnified in a culture "where there is pressure to meet an unrealistic body size." If society should become less preoccupied with how women look, says Garfinkel, the disorders might well become less prevalent. "And if women are expected to be less thin," he adds, "I think we'll see the impact." After an increase in the 1970s and 1980s, Garfinkel says, the incidence of eating disorders has levelled off. Even so, about one to one-and-a-half percent of young women have serious cases of bulimia (binge-eating alternating with purging by vomiting or laxatives) and another less than one percent have anorexia nervosa.

5   As for Jenna, her plight is not about statistics but about memories, many of them painful. Naturally slim, she snacked when she studied and was panic-stricken to find herself weighing 120 pounds by the end of her senior year in high school. "I always felt rejected and hurt. I had extreme feelings that I felt weren't right and I found that when I wasn't eating, I didn't feel them." So began a year of eating less and exercising strenuously. "Then there came a point where I stopped eating and if I did eat anything, I purged. I never thought not eating wasn't normal. I actually felt healthier." After leaving the hospital, Jenna says, "those overwhelming feelings started coming back," so she once again stopped eating. Her parents and the group at St. Paul's have offered support. "Not eating is just a way of numbing out your feelings," Jenna acknowledges. "If you're too busy thinking about calories and food, you don't have time to think about other issues, like rejection and anxiety and anger."

6   Those emotional issues are widely shared by anorexics. Shannon, who also requested anonymity, has one week left of her three-month outpatient program at St. Paul's. She now

sees that becoming obsessed with food, weight and body image was a way to avoid dealing with more subtle problems: a lack of assertiveness and fear of failure and disappointment. Having anorexia, she claims, "is like living in a fake world. When you're not eating, you feel like you're running away from whatever it is and staying ahead of the game. Like drugs, it's a different way to cope."

7　　For Mackenzie Stroh, 23, family problems, since resolved, likely played a part in her lengthy battle with anorexia and bulimia. She spent eight months in a women's centre in Calgary, where her weight dropped to 65 pounds. She attempted suicide by overdosing on pills. After moving to Victoria, she sought counselling: "I started to enjoy everything too much not to want to get better." Now a student at Emily Carr College of Art and Design in Vancouver, Stroh has been in recovery for almost two years.

8　　Across the country, hundreds of women are trapped by an illness that mocks them with illusion while it devastates their bodies. Hundreds of others, like Jenna, are trying to break free. "I've hit a real wall," she says, "but I want to face everything that I'm feeling." For anorexics, that is the road to freedom.

VOCABULARY

1. "She sprawls on the couch." (para. 1) Define *sprawls* in your own words.

_____

2. Find a word in paragraph 1 that means "infirm or weakened."

_____

3. What is a synonym for *plight?* (para. 5)

_____

4. Find a word in paragraph 8 that means "makes fun of."

_____

READING COMPREHENSION

1. How does the writer introduce the topic in this essay, and why is this introduction style effective?

_____

_____

_____

_____

2. According to Adrienne Webb, what are some causes of eating disorders? List them in point form.

_____

_____

_____

_____

3. The ideal looks promoted by popular culture are unrealistic, and may contribute to the increase in eating disorders. What evidence does Webb put forth to prove this point?

_____

_____

_____

_____

4. List the experts that the author quotes from to prove her point.

_____   _____

_____

5. According to the article, what can people with eating disorders do to free themselves from their illness?

_____

_____

_____

_____

DISCUSSION

1. Have you felt pressure to be thin? What, precisely, has made you feel this way?

2. Adrienne Webb proposes a solution to the problem: _those with eating disorders must face everything that they're feeling_. Each year in Canada and the U.S., eating disorders claim thousands of lives. How realistic is Webb's solution to the problem? Why?

3. What, in your opinion, could also be done to combat the problem of eating disorders? Come up with specific, workable solutions.

# Writing Tips

Doing Research

Presenting a good argument is not an easy task. Sometimes you may "feel" that something is wrong, but because you are not very well informed, your arguments about the issue are weak and unconvincing.

Research Several Sources

In order to properly argue your position, you must develop a certain expertise in your subject. Not only is it useful to know how those who agree with you structure and argue their position, but it is also valuable to read articles by those who disagree with you. By going to a variety of sources, you can:

- broaden your knowledge about that issue.
- reflect on the depth of your own feelings about the issue.
- find more extensive historical background information about the subject.
- test your view against opposing arguments.
- determine the strengths of opposing arguments.
- find relevant facts, statistics and examples that support your views.

Verify Internet "Facts"

Most of you are adept at using the Internet, and it can be a valuable source of material for a research project. However, you must verify that the source of the information is legitimate. Remember, anyone can write pretty much anything on the Internet and present the information as factual. That doesn't mean that facts on the Internet are true.

For example, you need statistics regarding gun control. You find statistics posted by "People who love guns," more statistics in an article that was in *Maclean's* magazine, and a page filled with the opinions of various people. The magazine article was probably checked by editors for the veracity of the facts. The other two sources are not necessarily reliable.

Make sure that you acknowledge your source when you use material from the Internet.

Quote Relevant Ideas

When you research a subject, the goal is not to simply take arguments from a variety of authors and stick them together. Only borrow ideas that are relevant and useful in illustrating your points, and don't quote others simply for the sake of quoting others. When you do your final written or oral version, always remember to credit each author whose idea you borrow.

Carefully Organize Your Ideas

The way that you organize your topic is extremely important. Obviously, if you begin with your best argument, you will quickly lose momentum in your presentation.

Build your case in an organized and logical way, and make sure that you use well-planned transitions so that your readers can see the relationship of various parts of the argument, and they can observe how you have linked your arguments together to make an effective whole.

Writing Suggestion

Write a research essay about one of the following topics. Try to find at least two other articles about that subject before you write your essay.

1. Divorce is clearly harmful for children.
2. "Marriage for life" is unrealistic.
3. Couples should (or should not) stay together for the sake of the children.
4. Thin models in advertising contribute (or don't contribute) to eating disorders.
5. Our society is overly obsessed with beauty.

Speaking Suggestion

Have a "round-table" discussion about any of the above topics. Make sure that everybody has a chance to express his or her point of view. Students could be grouped in teams and the conclusions could be shared with the rest of the class.

10 Planning a Debate

T he following readings, which discuss controversial issues, could become source material for a debate.

Reading 10.1

The Preoccupation with Tears
by Charles Gordon

When Marilyn Monroe divorced Joe Dimaggio, the news media filmed her tearful face as she left the courthouse. When an airplane exploded over the ocean near New York, several major North American magazines depicted huddled, grieving relatives standing on the shore looking out at the scene of the disaster.

In the following article, Charles Gordon examines the media's obsession with emotional moments.

1   Try to remember the last time you watched a television news program without once seeing a camera tightly focused on someone's sadness. More and more, the media treat grief as big news.

2   Each horror in the world finds its corresponding horror in the news media. You will be all too familiar with the routine by now. The relative of a victim is speaking. The camera moves in, closer than usual. A tear falls. The camera finds it. Switch to another station: the same clip, the same tear. Switch again: a funeral, people are weeping, in close-up. Pick up the newspaper: there's a photograph of the same scene. If the picture is not as clear as it was on television, the words under the picture will make sure you know that tears were being shed. The obsession with tears is not thwarted by their absence. "There are no tears behind the dark glasses," began one story about a relative of an Air-India victim.

3   No one would object to tears on their television screens, tears in their newspapers, if it were not for the nagging suspicion that the newspapers and television networks are actively looking for them, searching for grief to bring into the living rooms of the nation. The sorrow hunt makes ghouls of the news media, exploiting both those who are grieving and those who are watching.

4   Does anybody enjoy it? Not likely. Ask any newspaper photographer or television cameraman how happy he is to be clicking away among the mourners. Ask any reporter how much he enjoys asking unhappy people how unhappy they are. And ask the subjects if it helps them deal with their grief to have people taking their pictures and asking them questions. As for the consumers of this news—if news is what it is—many are unhappy too. It offends them to be eavesdropping on the worst moment in another person's life.

5   So why inflict cameras on the mourners, the mourning on the public? "The public has a right to know," is one stock answer. "We don't make the news, we just report it," is another. No one will argue with the first one. We do have a right. But in the case of grieving relatives, we *already know*.

6   No one has to tell us that when innocent people die their relatives grieve. It would be news if they did not. That, in fact, is one definition of news—something unexpected; something new. This definition gives rise to the hard-boiled newsman's defence of all the negative, depressing and anxiety-producing stories in the paper: "It's not news," he will tell you, "when a plane doesn't crash." Think about that the next time someone says, "We don't make the news, we just report it." If it is not noteworthy when a plane doesn't crash, why is it news that people grieve when one does?

7   The irony of the media's obsession with grief is that grief is *not* news, by the commonly accepted definitions of the term. It is not unexpected. It is human nature, and human nature is not news. People only make news when they go against human nature—when they behave in unpredictable ways, by being unusually brave, vicious, lucky or silly.

8   Grief is not news, then. Grief is spectacle. By making a spectacle out of grief, the media cheapen it, trivialize it. The tears of the victim's mother may be followed by the tears of the lottery winner. The question is why anyone thinks we need spectacle, why anyone thinks emotion is news.

9   Somebody thinks so; there is no doubt about that. Watch the news coverage of the House of Commons. The politician who yells, the one who displays his anger for the camera is the one who makes the evening news. Never mind what he is yelling about. The anger is the thing. The alderman who blows up at a council meeting is the one who gets the headlines. Did he blow up over a matter of any importance? Never mind. Watch the sports news. You will see far more of John McEnroe having tantrums than you will of him playing tennis. If a fight breaks out in any sporting event other than boxing, and perhaps hockey, the fight will figure in the highlights clip, even though the fight had nothing to do with the outcome of the game.

10   The people who decide that emotion is news must think that emotion is important to us, the readers and viewers. They must think that we need emotion in our newspapers and on

our television screens. And perhaps some of us do. Perhaps there is so little real emotion in our lives that we are thrilled by it whenever it is given to us by the media. Note that performers who at least *seem* to be emotional—Remember Johnny Ray? Remember Judy Garland?—often attain enormous popularity. Note the success of soap opera, professional wrestling, *Love Story* and any number of drippy songs.

11   The more reserved a nation is, runs one theory, the more vicarious emotion it needs in its mass media. In support of that theory, take as Exhibit A the British people and as Exhibit B the excitable British tabloid press. Canadians think of themselves as more reserved than the Americans, less reserved than the British. Our newspapers are not particularly sensational, our television news is not particularly lurid. But more and more our news media are less concerned with the content of the news than with the way people feel about it. This is defended on the grounds of giving the people what they want.

12   Whether the people really want it or not, it does happen to be easier to provide. Journalists do not have to work as hard to explain people's reactions to events as they do to explain the events themselves. To analyse a federal budget takes skill and depth of understanding. Neither is required to show people being angry about the budget. You stick the microphone into their faces and ask them how mad they are.

13   It is less immediately productive to stick a microphone into a budget's face. The budget is not mad. It is not even happy. It is just there, its columns of figures sending out confusing and sometimes contradictory signals. Many reporters have the skill and the depth of understanding necessary to translate those signals into English, to show what a cut in Column A means to the economy of Northern Alberta. But few reporters are encouraged to do so. For most news executives, tears are enough. Yet in the long run the analysis is far more important, potentially far more helpful than full and comprehensive coverage of someone's rage.

14   The same goes for full and comprehensive coverage of someone's grief. The grief is real. We know it; we sympathize with it. But if someone tries to tell us that the exploitation of the grief of others is being done on our behalf, we should say: "No thanks. Leave those people alone."

VOCABULARY

Guess the meaning of the verbs in Column A by matching them with the possible definitions in Column B. Write the letter of the matching definition in the space provided. The number in parentheses indicates the paragraph where the word can be found.

Column A			Column B	
1. *switch*	(2)	_____	**A.**	to feel deep sorrow
2. *weep*	(2)	_____	**B.**	to cry
3. *thwart*	(2)	_____	**C.**	to change from one to another
4. *eavesdrop*	(4)	_____	**D.**	to frustrate or impede
5. *grieve*	(6)	_____	**E.**	to secretly listen to someone

Find the noun in the text that each of the following adjectives modify. The paragraph number is indicated in parentheses. Find a synonym for each adjective.

Adjective	Noun that is modified	Synonym for the adjective
6. *nagging* (3)		
7. *hard-boiled* (6)		
8. *drippy* (10)		
9. *lurid* (11)		

10. Find a noun in paragraph 9 that means "a childish fit of anger." _____

READING COMPREHENSION

1. According to Charles Gordon, what is the definition of "news"?

_____

2. Why does Gordon think that grief is not news?

_____

_____

3. In the text "The Preoccupation With Tears," Charles Gordon:
   a) identifies the problem
   b) proves that there is a problem
   c) suggests a solution to the problem

The problem is "the media's obsession with grief." How does Gordon prove that there is a problem? Paraphrase some of his arguments:

_____

_____

_____

_____

_____

What does Gordon propose as a solution to the problem?

_____

_____

_____

How feasible, or realistic, is Gordon's solution to the problem? Explain your answer.

_____

_____

_____

DISCUSSION

1. Why do journalists tend to turn their cameras towards the enraged politician or the weeping relative? Do you think that people need emotion in newspapers and on their screens? Why or why not?

2. Gordon writes about the media's obsession with all types of emotion, from rage, to childish temper tantrums, to deep sorrow and grief. Is one type of emotion more legitimate to exploit than another?

3. If you were a news editor, which of the following images would you play on tonight's news? Which would you refuse to air on the grounds that it is exploitative? Explain your reasons.
    *   a crowd screaming in anger in front of an embassy
    *   hockey players involved in a brutal fist fight during a hockey game
    *   a man shooting at a crowd in a fast-food restaurant
    *   relatives of a deceased celebrity weeping in front of the coffin
    *   a politician yelling at another politician in the House of Commons
    *   a mother sobbing at the news that her child has just died
    *   a local politician sneering and calling an opponent a cruel name
    *   a family's tears of joy just after a child is rescued from a dangerous situation
    *   a political extremist setting himself on fire to make a point

4. Divide into categories types of emotions that you would film, and those that you wouldn't.

5. During the next week, find some examples of photos that depict an emotional moment. The photos can be taken from newspapers or magazines. Decide which photos are exploitative. In groups, decide if any of the photos should not have been published, and explain why.

Reading 10.2

Biceps in a Bottle
by James Deacon

Advertising is created with one goal in mind: sell the product. Unfortunately, in an effort to sell, advertisers like to distort reality. For example, smokers, who are really harming their bodies, are often depicted outdoors doing athletic activities.

In recent years, thin, yet extremely muscular, men have been used to promote products. In fact, "sexy" men are becoming as prevalent on billboards as "sexy" women. How vulnerable are young men to this type of advertising?

1   He is the new man. His state-of-the-art physique is displayed on everything from billboards and television shows to dance-music videos and the fashion pages of men's

magazines. He is young and muscular, but eschews the steel-belted-radial appearance of competitive body-builders. His is the lean and hungry "cut" look as exemplified by Marky Mark, the rapper turned Calvin Klein model. Bulging biceps, chiselled chest and washboard stomach are his fashion accessories, amply exposed over low-riding jeans. As portrayed in pop culture, the new man is Saturday night-primed, his hard body a turn-on to women and a threat to other men. And that is precisely what a lot of teenage boys want. But their bodies are still developing, so the only quick way to achieve that ideal look is by turning to anabolic steroids to get what nature did not supply. "You see anyone in high school who is big—has ripped mass, the curl in the bicep, the veins—and you know he's on it," says a teenage steroid user who asks to be called Joe. "He's juiced."

2   Steroids, once exclusive to elite athletes and hard-core body-builders, are now the elixirs of young males' vanity. The muscle-building substances, generally used by veterinarians on animals, are widely available to Canadian high-school students through networks of other athletes or at gyms. They are costly: a five-week cycle of use costs $600 or more. Yet according to a 1993 study commissioned by the Ottawa-based Canadian Centre for Drug-Free Sport, about 83,000 Canadians between the ages of 11 and 18 now use steroids, and nearly half of those are solely concerned with improving body image. Experts link the phenomenon to the recent exploitation of "beefcake" to sell everything from fragrances to floor cleaners. "These guys are out there with really distorted views of what they should look like," says Dr. Arthur Blouin, a psychologist at the Ottawa Civic Hospital who is studying the similarities between steroid abuse and eating disorders. "They are willing to risk the side-effects of steroids to avoid the negative perception that they are too small and weak."

3   Tom (not his real name) agrees. A decent student and good athlete, he began weight training to keep fit after breaking his leg. He liked how it made him look but, he says, "I wanted more size, faster." Last summer, encouraged by a training partner, he began taking steroids, both in pill form and by injections into the muscles of his buttocks. When school resumed in September, he says, "I got a huge response, from guys and girls. I was sort of shocked at first, but after a while, I began to like it." He found, however, that when he went off the drugs he lost weight rapidly—much the way sprinter Ben Johnson did when he stopped his own steroid use. Deeply depressed, Tom would buy more and begin another cycle. "You might be able to dodge the physical side-effects for a long time if you know what you're doing," he says. "But you can't avoid what steroids do to your head."

4   Tom and others like him confirm that, in part, their body-image obsession is a response to the depiction of men as sex objects in mainstream media. "Kids see the well-built guys on TV, getting the girls and the respect from the guys," says Tom, "and they want that, too." But in their zeal to look great, steroid users risk a far worse fate than a skinny body. Steroid use commonly leads to prolific outbreaks of acne on the upper back, baldness, shrunken testicles, reduced sexual drive, heavier beards, a puffy face and depression. Prolonged abuse can cause heart and liver disorders, growth of tumors and damage to the endocrine system. Just as dangerous are what users call steroid rages. "Your whole mentality changes," says Joe. "You

go from an intelligent, normal guy to someone who resorts to beating people up if they don't agree with you. It's a totally physical mentality, and very aggressive."

5   Furthermore, novice users don't realize that a large percentage of black-market steroids are cut with other substances to improve dealers' profits, says Vancouver-based RCMP Const. Keith Pearce. In a raid on a Vancouver dealer's home last March, members of Pearce's detachment seized liquid anabolic steroids that were mixed with Armor-All, a compound used to shine car dashboards. Metropolitan Toronto police Sgt. Savas Kyriacou says that the vast majority of users do not consult physicians, and instead rely on information from people in the gyms. "Like any type of street-level drug, steroids get cut every time they change hands," Kyriacou says. "A lot of these kids are injecting themselves with chemicals that are even worse than the steroids."

6   Starting out, of course, young users see only the benefits. "I'd be at a club or something and no one would mess with me," Tom says. "And girls were more friendly—I got more dates." But that high can be short-lived. Joe stopped taking the drugs because he could no longer work out after seriously injuring his shoulder. Now 19 and getting ready to begin university, he says he has gained perspective. "If I hadn't had the injury, I would probably still be taking them now," he says. "But that could just as easily have kept heading me down the road to self-destruction. I mean, would they find me dead of a heart attack in my dorm room some day, with a needle sticking out of my ass? I don't know." He is glad, he says, that he never found out.

VOCABULARY

1. Find a word in paragraph 1 that means "to avoid or refrain from." _____

2. Find a different word in paragraph 3 that means "to avoid." _____

3. Find a synonym for the word "exemplified." (para. 1) _____

4. At the end of paragraph 1, a teenager named Joe said, "He's juiced." What does he mean?

_____

5. "Experts link the phenomenon to the recent exploitation of 'beefcake' to sell everything from fragrances to floor cleaners." Define *beefcake*.

_____

6. What is the definition of *elixir* as it is used in paragraph 2? _____
   a) a substance capable of changing metal into gold
   b) a cure-all
   c) a sweetened alcoholic mixture used as medicine

READING COMPREHENSION

1. What is the problem discussed in the article?

_____

2. What are some examples used as evidence that there is a problem?

_____

_____

_____

_____

_____

3. Why do boys take steroids, according to James Deacon?

_____

_____

_____

4. What are some of the problems associated with steroid use?

_____

_____

_____

_____

DISCUSSION

1. In his article, "Biceps in a Bottle," James Deacon looks at the problem of steroid abuse. He doesn't, however, offer solutions to the problem. What could be done to stop steroid use among youths?

2. Do you know anyone who uses steroids? Do you think that advertising really alters the way that boys and young men see themselves? Why do you think most boys would use steroids?

3. Canadian runner Ben Johnson has implied that the best Olympic athletes need steroids to win. In Johnson's case this was true, for his performance deteriorated without the performance-enhancing drugs. Every day new performance-enhancing drugs are invented for athletes in a never-ending attempt to outwit drug tests. How realistic are drug bans in athletic events? What could be done to solve the problem of drug use in sports?

The Body Builders

by Patricia Chisolm, with Sharon Doyle Driedger and Joe Chidley

We have a myriad of clichés claiming that beauty doesn't matter, such as "beauty is only skin deep" or "beauty is in the eye of the beholder." Most people would deny that beauty is of great importance, yet men and women are lining up to have their bodies cosmetically altered.

The following article looks at our current obsession with cosmetic surgery. As you read, highlight the types of cosmetic surgery. In preparation for the reading comprehension questions, you could also highlight positive and negative effects of cosmetic surgery.

1 Come on now, is it really worth it?

2 As Toronto cosmetic surgeon John Taylor shoves a huge needle through his patient's soft cheek, from jawline to eye, the line of the syringe stands out under the skin like a tent pole. To an untrained observer, it looks more like mutilation than beautification. But the 55-year-old woman, sedated and still conscious, is only slightly perturbed by these preliminaries and the deep surgical cuts that will soon separate her face from its moorings. In fact, she is downright sporting, chatting with Taylor as he slices, snips, and sews. After all, she is a veteran: the partial face-lift and minor adjustment to the tip of her nose that she is having today—for about $3,700—will go nicely with the brow lift and eyelid lift she has already undergone. She feels a bit guilty about spending so much on herself, but figures that the amount is not really out of line when compared with more conventional luxuries. "It'll last longer than a holiday," she reasons.

3 While a nurse and anesthetist hover nearby, soothing harp music wafts through the sunny operating room in Taylor's private clinic. There is very little blood amid the glistening fat and muscle, a result of advanced anesthetic techniques that will also minimize nausea and postoperative grogginess. Two hours later, a line of neat black sutures marks a curving wound that runs beside the hairline from earlobe to eye. Beside it stretches a smooth expanse where crow's feet and jowls reigned before. By tomorrow there will be some heavy bruising around the cheeks and neck, but within two weeks only her hairdresser and cosmetician will know for sure. And that, the woman says, is exactly the way she wants it. "This is psychosurgery," says Taylor, who is president-elect of the Canadian Society of Plastic Surgeons. "It's done for psychological reasons."

4 Quite a concept. Smooth out the cheeks, pump up the breasts, suck off the spare tire, and what gets fixed? THE BRAIN. In the United States, an estimated $3.5 billion was spent on cosmetic surgery in 1994, up from $2.6 billion in 1992. While similar statistics are not kept in Canada, surgeons say the increase is roughly parallel to the 35-percent jump south of the border. And a growing proportion of patients are men, getting everything from hair transplants to penis enlargements; the number of male clients has more than doubled over the past two decades, to between a quarter and a third of the total. Some are aging

businessmen newly sensitive to the importance of image. Too sensitive, in fact, to go public—although at least one Canadian billionaire has had a hair transplant, while the chief executive officers of two large Canadian corporations have had eyelid lifts.

5   Many Hollywood types, on the other hand, have let it all hang out. Canada's Pamela Anderson Lee, of the TV beach-show *Baywatch*, and Demi Moore, star of the new film *Striptease*, are famed for upping their market value along with their bra size. In the process, they have also pointed up the pay-offs of looking good. "Attractiveness attracts," says Anthony Synnott, professor of sociology at Concordia University in Montreal and author of *The Body Social: Symbolism, Self and Society*. "Beautiful people are considered more intelligent, sexier, happier and more trustworthy than other people. It's just astonishing."

6   But cosmetic surgery is not like fooling around with a bottle of hair dye or getting a set of fake fingernails. The procedures are invasive, the recovery sometimes painful—and mistakes, while not common, can be difficult or impossible to correct. Breast implants may rupture, noses sink inward, and smiles turn unnaturally tight. People who merely wanted fat vacuumed from their thighs have died, while balding men have found themselves sporting new hair in symmetrical rows like tree farms. And then there are the junkies, the ones who go under the knife time and again, gradually altering their faces beyond recognition or developing an eerie youthfulness: Michael Jackson and Cher bear only a passing resemblance to their younger selves. Some observers see not enhanced beauty but the signs of a spreading malaise. "The cultural emphasis on a part, like a face or breast, convinces people that it is their whole identity," says Stephen Katz, a sociologist at Trent University in Peterborough, Ont. "To have plastic surgery, you have to think of your body as an object. It's a kind of social madness."

7   The phenomenon is all the more startling given the costs: cosmetic surgery, with rare exceptions, is not covered by public health care and it does not come cheap. A new bosom ranges from $3,000 to $6,000, while a nose job costs about $4,000 and a hair transplant comes as high as $60,000. Yet plastic surgeons say their patients come from virtually all classes and occupations, from actors to real estate agents to waitresses. And while the first of the baby boomers are turning 50 only this year—too young to create lineups for lifts and liposuction—forecasters predict that in this area as well, the boomers may soon push demand to historic highs.

8   People who have had cosmetic surgery often report that their lives are rejuvenated along with their faces or bodies: there may be new lovers, a promotion, more success with clients. Synnott, for one, says that concern with appearance is not entirely bad. "People have been consumed with the notion of beauty since Plato," he says. "It's a normal part of being human." Problems arise, he says, when beauty is the only or primary yardstick of accomplishment. "It's very rough on people who are less attractive. They can be discriminated against in areas like employment, and it has nothing to do with merit."

9   Few know that better than middle-aged men, downsized out of a job and facing stiff competition from younger smooth-cheeked candidates. "Experience and competence don't

count for much any more, because there are so many competent people out there," says Toronto image consultant Roz Usheroff, who works with major outplacement firms like Price Waterhouse. "People aren't being hired and promoted because they are better. It's because they look current."

10   Most men, especially businessmen, would not admit to an eyelid lift, liposuction or hair transplant. Often, though, there is not much more behind male motivation than that biblical bad guy, vanity. Philip Rodgers, a 52-year-old Vancouver real estate agent who recently had a tummy tuck and liposuction, says he only considered the surgery after diets and exercise refused to budge an intractable bulge around his waist. "Every time I looked down, I saw this thing that I hated," recalls Rodgers, who is divorced and the father of two adult children.

11   Surgery cut away about two pounds of loose flesh and vacuumed off a small amount of fat. Rodgers says he is thrilled with his flat midriff, even though his current partner had repeatedly assured him he had nothing to worry about and no one notices any difference when he is fully clothed. The main thing, Rodgers says, is that his body now reflects his inner image of himself. "In the past, just being a man was enough to feel powerful and attractive," he muses. "But in the late 20th century, new ideals of beauty are compelling men to have plastic surgery, too."

12   Some are willing to risk impotence or even death to realize personal fantasies or virility. Men with $4,200 and a high pain threshold can have their penises stretched or widened. One of the procedures, performed by only about 100 surgeons worldwide, uses cuts at the base of the penis to release a section normally hidden inside the body. The penis is then stretched with weights or elastic for about six months. The increase can be as much as 2 1/2 inches—and as little as nothing. Widening—a separate procedure—is done using skin and fat grafts, usually taken from the lower abdomen and sewn onto the shaft. But here, too, there are possible side-effects, including loss of sensation, infection and scarring.

13   Scary perhaps, and Toronto plastic surgeon Robert Stubbs, who pioneered both procedures in Canada, is quick to warn that some patients report the operation was a disaster that ruined their lives. In fact, Stubbs says he turns away about 75 percent of the men who contact him, often for psychological reasons. Yet Stubbs can barely keep up with the demand for his services. And on a lean, healthy patient, he can get some "phenomenal results," he says. "This is man's sex symbol," says Stubbs. "He perceives himself, and others perceive him, based on the size of his organ."

14   For a man, there is also the matter of the hair on his head. More than 50 percent of men experience significant hair loss by the time they enter their fifth decade, and many believe it sends a false signal that their best years are behind them. Ironically, male pattern baldness is caused by a byproduct of the male hormone, testosterone. But that doesn't matter to those with extremely high foreheads and the money to spend on transplants—a procedure that involves relocating the patient's own healthy hair follicles from one part of the scalp to another. "The question is not why men do it, but why they don't," says Toronto surgeon Walter Unger. "If you could look 10 to 15 years younger, why wouldn't you?"

15   Unger, 57, counts celebrities and wealthy businessmen among his clients, and draws more than half of his patients from outside Canada. But he admits only to operating on Mel Lastman, the flamboyant mayor of the Toronto suburb of North York, as well as repairing another doctor's work on U.S. Senator Joseph Biden (while disavowing his rumored responsibility for Elton John's unsightly rows). His fees are among the highest in the business—about $10,000 per session, with most men requiring about six sessions. "In two to three months, the new hair will appear," says Unger. "At first it will be fine and short, then it slowly grows in—it just looks like a clock going backwards." That is precisely what Dan Nault, a 29-year-old salesman from New Jersey, had in mind. "I have a young face and I didn't want to look old," says Nault, sitting in Unger's operating room while two assistants build a helmet of white bandages over his freshly punctured scalp. "I want to be able to drive down the road with the wind in my hair."

16   And that, in a way, is what cosmetic surgery is all about: maximum fun, the sooner the better. Many younger patients are using one of the hottest new techniques, laser surgery, to smooth out fine lines and remove skin discolorations of virtually all kinds. Toronto dermatologist and laser surgeon Daniel Schachter says that his laser practice has grown significantly over the past few years as the equipment has improved, leading to more uses, greater accuracy and less scarring. Although the technology is not fully understood, scientists believe the light from certain types of lasers is absorbed by pigmented skin, but not surrounding areas. Others vaporize the water in all the skin cells they touch, destroying the cell, and in the process removing a layer of skin: they are used for smoothing out fine lines and other surface imperfections.

17   One morning at Laserderm, a clinic devoted entirely to laser surgery, Schachter uses a variety of lasers to erase a tattoo, greatly reduce a disfiguring birthmark and burn away acne scars. "Wear the glasses or you'll go blind," he casually warns a visitor as he prepares to zap the freckles from the arm of a young woman. Tiny flashes of intense light pulse from the high-tech black wand, the latest in so-called Q-switched ruby lasers. With each pulse, a small, slightly raised red circle forms over the offending freckle, and soon the woman's arm resembles a mass of bee stings. Despite a local anesthetic in the form of a gooey ointment, she winces a little towards the end of a treatment she badly wanted. "I didn't like the unevenness," she says of her freckles, explaining why she was spending hundreds of dollars, spread over several sessions, to achieve uniformly white arms.

18   Such is the cry heard from countless numbers of the surgically enhanced: "This is bugging me, please fix it!" Some wait a year or two before seeking help, some wait 20, but the overwhelming majority—97 percent—are happy with the results, surgeons say. Then there is utter dreamland. Henry Shimizu, an Edmonton plastic surgeon, says he has operated on several patients who wanted to look like Elvis Presley. One, a performer, now places highly in Elvis look-alike contests. "There are major differences between Elvis's face and his face," Shimizu says. "But he was happy to get whatever we could do to help him get as close as possible."

19   Many women feel the same way about the perfect bustline. While some seek breast reduction, far more opt for enlargement. "The first group are women who have had children and their breasts don't look the way they used to," says Dr. Richard Warren, chief of plastic surgery at the University of British Columbia. "The second group are young women, often single." The women are still lining up for surgery even though breast implants (especially those filled with silicone) have been blamed for symptoms ranging from rock-like hardening of the breast to immune system disorders. An avalanche of lawsuits in the United States in the early 1990s failed to prove conclusively that the implants were dangerous. Still, most are now made of silicone bags filled with saline solution.

20   Such is the appeal of an ample figure that even botched jobs can end happily ever after. One 28-year-old Toronto bartender and part-time university student had to cope with sharp pain on one side immediately after having breast implants inserted last March. For two months, her doctor refused to take her complaints seriously. During that time, other surgeons confirmed her suspicions that the implant had ruptured and had to be removed. "It had rolled up into a ball in the bottom of my breast," she recalls. "I had a C cup on one side and nothing on the other side. I went through hell."

21   For awhile, she felt trapped. No other doctors would touch her, for fear of becoming embroiled in a lawsuit, and they directed her back to the original surgeon. Desperate, she finally agreed and he repaired the damage. She is now ecstatic about her new breasts. "They look totally natural—they don't look like coconuts," she says. "I feel feminine and sexy—I can't explain it—it's amazing."

22   She was surprised at the difference in how male and female friends reacted to her new assets. Most of the women were congratulatory, but some of the men have questioned why she did it. She says that attitude mystifies her, since most of the same men frequently point out—and admire—large-breasted women. Besides, there are other payoffs—tips from customers have increased by about 15 percent. "When I leave at the end of the night, I come home with $200 in my pocket because someone was looking at my breasts," she says. "It pays for school."

23   Above the neck, esthetic ideas are somewhat different. The urge is to make large features less noticeable, such as protruding ears and, especially, noses. That kind of work, many surgeons say, is where the art comes in. Peter Adamson, president-elect of the American Academy of Facial Plastic and Reconstructive Surgery, practically cringes at the commonly used phrase, nose job. "It's like being at a dinner party and saying, 'I'm having a hash job,'" he protests. Rhinoplasty, the correct term, is the procedure most commonly performed by head and neck surgeons, and it is one of the most difficult to get right. Problems can include removal of too much bone and cartilage, leaving a bridge or tip that is too narrow. But the risks may be worth it. According to Adamson, a good rhinoplasty can help teenagers stop obsessing about their faces or encourage shy adults to enter into relationships or pursue new jobs.

24   Then there is the in-between crowd. They have no major facial or body problems, are too young for a full face-lift, but well past the bloom of youth. Many are taking what surgeons

call the à la carte approach: a small tuck here, a zap with the laser there, and a 40-year-old can pass for 30. Later, when gravity really begins to take its toll, they can have more aggressive procedures without giving themselves away.

25   Lloyd Carlsen, who operates the only cosmetic surgery hospital in North America—in Woodbridge, 40 km north of Toronto—as well as a popular clinic in the Cayman Islands, says that new techniques are particularly useful for those on the threshold of middle age. Endoscopy, for instance, uses slender probes fitted with tiny lenses, inserted through relatively small incisions. "A 38- or 39-year-old woman who has sort of a sag in the mid-portion of the face but her neck is fine, and she just wants that sag brought up—she's a good candidate for an endoscopic face-lift," Carlsen says. "But 50-year-old patients are not, because they have skin that has to be removed."

26   Carlsen, who opened his Woodbridge hospital in 1971 when cosmetic surgery was still a hush-hush topic, also says that resurfacing with lasers can "tide over" a person in his late 30s for six or seven years before a face-lift. Dermabrasion and chemical peels—older techniques that use sand and acid, respectively, to smooth out fine lines by removing the top layer of skin—might also be appropriate, he says, depending on skin type. In addition, some wrinkles can be temporarily plumped up with collagen or lips made fashionably full with implants made from the high-tech fabric Gortex—the same stuff used to make waterproof, breathable clothing. Botox, a drug made from the highly toxic botulism bacteria, can be injected into brow furrows, temporarily smoothing out frown lines by paralyzing forehead muscles. That treatment, which was developed by Canadian doctors, lasts about six months.

27   But when the time comes to gut the existing structure and rebuild, there is no escaping major surgery. Carlsen says that older couples like to come to his Cayman Islands clinic together, turning their dual face-lifts into a Caribbean holiday far from prying eyes. Some wives travelling on their own also prefer the clinic's privacy—and distance from disapproving husbands. Others, like Del and C.R. Dilkie, wear their new faces like a badge. Del, an Edmonton fashion retailer, had her first face-lift and chemical peel in 1986, when she was 56. "The happiest moment of my life was when the peel fell off my upper lip and chin about a week after the operation," she recalls. "I knew I looked 10 to 15 years younger. I was proud to tell my age because I looked so good." She is equally thrilled with a second face-lift and tummy tuck she had last October, and she has no intention of ever accepting the ravages of time: "If I live to be 100, I'll probably have two more face-lifts. If you are 100 and you look 70 or 75, isn't that nice?"

28   Her husband, who manages rental properties, is no stranger to the knife either. He underwent a nose job in 1966, a full face-lift 10 years ago, a chemical peel in 1994, a second face-lift last year. "It's the best thing since sliced bread," C.R. says. "Anything you can do to make yourself feel better—do it. Never mind spending money on drinking and smoking—spend it on a face-lift."

29   It is hard to argue with satisfied customers. But there are those who warn that turning to cosmetic surgery in search of self-esteem is a dead end. "People end up not living in their lives, because they aren't living in their bodies," argues Trent University's Katz. "Wrinkles are

a sign that you've lived, loved, had experiences. That's something to be proud of." Warren, the UBC doctor, acknowledges that cosmetic surgery may not be the best way to deal with insecurities about appearance. "It's too bad we can't overcome it with our cerebrum, but it is just part of human nature," he says. Maybe—although some people certainly do overcome it, without benefit of a knife. Others—like real estate agent Rodgers, who had a tummy tuck and liposuction—take a middle road. "I'm a bald-headed little man, but I would never do anything to mask the natural aging of my face," Rodgers says. "I like being 52—I wouldn't be young again. I like the fact that I've acquired knowledge and experience. When I look in the mirror, I like what I see." In the end, surgery or no surgery, who can argue with that?

VOCABULARY

1. Find a word in paragraph 2 that means *bothered*. _____

2. On the face, draw "crow's feet and jowls." (para. 3)

Guess the meaning of the words in Column A by matching them with the possible definitions in Column B. Write the letter of the matching definition in the space provided. The number in parentheses indicates the paragraph where the word can be found.

Column A			Column B	
3. *grogginess*	(3)	_____	**A.**	a distended part
4. *eerie*	(6)	_____	**B.**	a pained facial expression
5. *bulge*	(10)	_____	**C.**	bizarre, frightening
6. *wince*	(17)	_____	**D.**	state of being weak or unsteady
7. *plump up*	(26)	_____	**E.**	ridges between eyebrows
8. *furrows*	(26)	_____	**F.**	to fatten

READING COMPREHENSION

1. What are some of the mistakes that can occur with cosmetic surgery?

_____

_____

_____

2. What type of introduction does the author use? (descriptive, narrative, historical background or a combination)

_____

_____

_____

3. What are some of the positive aspects of cosmetic surgery, according to the author?

_____

_____

_____

4. What are some of the negative aspects of cosmetic surgery, according to the author?

_____

_____

_____

5. List the cosmetic surgery procedures mentioned in the article.

_____

_____

_____

DISCUSSION

1. In your opinion, does the author have a predominantly favorable, or unfavorable view of cosmetic surgery? Support your answer with evidence from the text.

2. According to Toronto surgeon Walter Unger, "If you could look 10 or 15 years younger, why wouldn't you?" Do you agree that most people would like to have cosmetic surgery at some point in their lives?

3. Our media currently equates beauty with youth. What other standards of beauty does our media perpetuate? How are these beauty standards unrealistic, or even dangerous?

4. Do you believe that "beautiful" people are happier? Do they have more successful lives?

5. In your opinion, what makes a person beautiful?

Speaking Tips

Preparing a Debate

Before you attempt a formal debate, you must prepare yourself very well. Robin Dick, an English teacher at College Lionel-Groulx in Quebec, compiled the following debate preparation strategy. If you are asked to argue for or against a proposal, here is an example of how you could do that:

The Issue: Ban smoking in all public places

If you agree with this proposal, you should do the following:

1. **You must first prove that there is a problem:**
   - Cigarette smoke damages people's health, including that of non-smokers.

2. **You must then propose your solution to the problem:**
   - Ban smoking in all public places.

3. **You must then prove that your solution is workable and effective:**
   - Only a total ban on smoking in public places will protect the health of non-smokers.
   - A ban on smoking would send the message that smoking is destructive, and maybe more smokers would quit the habit.
   - Smoking sections are ridiculous: smoke doesn't acknowledge boundaries.

If you are arguing against this proposal, you could do one or more of the following:

1. **You could deny that there is a problem:**
   - The amount of cigarette smoke in public places is minimal, and other types of air pollution are far more dangerous.

2. **You could show that there is a better solution to the problem:**
   - Instead of banning smoking in public places, cigarette taxes could be raised to discourage smoking.
   - Educate youth about the dangers of smoking.

3. **You could show that the solution is unrealistic:**
   - Bar and restaurant owners cannot be turned into "smoking police." It isn't fair to put them in that position.
   - A ban is unrealistic. Nobody would obey the ban, and there are not enough police to enforce such a ban.

It is important to give substantial arguments to support your point of view. Your opponent can destroy you if you rely only on hearsay or personal experience to prove your point.

Supporting Your View

Find support for your views from reliable sources. You could find the following types of evidence:

1. **Use Statistical support:** This can be used to support either side of a debate.

   With the "Smoking Ban" example, statistical evidence could be given to prove the dangers of second-hand smoke.

   The person arguing against the ban could find statistical evidence to prove that smokers wouldn't respect such bans.

2. **Quote respected sources:** Someone who has studied the issue could be considered a respected source. If you quote a source, let the audience know a little bit about WHO the source is.

   For example, if you quote a doctor about the terrible effects of smoking on non-smokers, it is more effective if the audience knows something about that doctor. If the doctor is a cancer specialist, and the doctor has spent years working with cancer patients, your quote carries more weight than if you simply say "Dr. Brown thinks..."

3. **Show logical consequences:** Every solution to a problem can carry long-term consequences with it.

   For example, if smoking is banned in all public places, the long-term consequences could be that we live in a police-state, with citizens reporting on fellow citizens.

4. **Make an analogy:** Compare the solution to the problem with something equally absurd.

   For example, if you think that a smoking ban is unworkable, you could claim that "banning smoking is like banning bad breath, because bad breath offends other people, or like banning insults, because insults hurt other people."

5. **Tell a true story:** If you have read about something related to the issue, you could tell that story to illustrate your point.

   For example, an American Airlines attendant was assaulted by a passenger when she tried to enforce a no-smoking ban on an airline. People who have to enforce such bans put themselves in unnecessary danger.

6. **Describe a personal experience:** You could talk about something that happened to you, or someone that you know, to illustrate your point.

   For example, if you have worked in a supposedly non-smoking environment, you could give anecdotal evidence to prove that people always find ways to cheat the bans. Maybe smoking was forbidden in your high school, but the washrooms were always filled with smoke.

Research your arguments thoroughly, and prepare counter-arguments. If you can predict what your opponent will probably say, you can more effectively rebut him or her.

Remember, it is important to be polite during a debate, and let your opponent express his or her views uninterrupted. You will have time to rebut your opponent's arguments.

Writing Suggestions

1. Write an informal opinion essay about any of the topics listed in the next section, Speaking Suggestions.

2. Write a researched essay about any of the topics listed in the next section, Speaking Suggestions.

Speaking Suggestions

Debate any of the following topics. Decide whether you agree or disagree with the statement. Your teacher may also give you additional topics to choose from. Make sure that you read the "preparing a debate" ideas in the Speaking Tips section of this chapter. Some of the following topics are related to readings in Chapters 8 or 9.

Prepare at least three solid arguments and prepare a strong closing statement that will rest in the minds of your audience.

1. Images depicting grief should be banned from all news media.
2. Unnaturally thin fashion models are dangerous for our society.
3. Steroids must be banned from professional athletic events.
4. Cosmetic surgery done for the sake of vanity is ridiculous.
5. Our society is overly obsessed with beauty.
6. Parents should stay together for the sake of the children.
7. Divorce is clearly harmful for children.
8. "Marriage for life" is unrealistic.
9. Wild animals should not be kept in captivity.
10. Experiments should not be done on animals.

11 Versions

Previous readings in this book were of the essay genre. "Versions" is a short story. The main difference between essays and short stories is that essays are written about real events, and short stories are about events that occur in the writer's imagination. However, what is true and what is fictional is not always clearly delineated.

Genni Gunn, a Vancouver-based writer of fiction and poetry, examines truth in her story "Versions." Truth and fiction may become intertwined in both life and literature!

Reading 11.1

Versions
by Genni Gunn

1   When I was two, my sister Marcia who was three and a half, lifted me up over a balcony railing and held me upside down by the ankles suspended two storeys above the street. When my mother walked into the room and saw this, she slipped off her shoes, took a deep breath and held it, then slowly crossed to the balcony so as not to startle Marcia.

2   Depending on my mother's mood, this part of the story is more or less elaborate. Sometimes she is wearing high heels (blue, to match her dress); other times Chinese red brocade slippers (and doesn't take them off); sometimes she is wearing black laced boots which would take too long to remove, so she has to walk on tiptoe very very slowly and carefully. The distance varies too: eight steps, fifteen, twenty-five. Sometimes, and this when she's feeling particularly dramatic, she is coming home from a friend's or the train station, and sees me from below. Then she must climb the stairs (often she can't find her key immediately and doesn't want to ring the bell in case Marcia is distracted).

3   The story always ends with my mother grabbing my ankles the exact moment Marcia lets go of them. And then, my mother leans back and says, "The trouble with Marcia is that she was so jealous," implying Marcia's entire life has been one enormous mistake (this being the first) made up of escalating small ones. A little like a novel, perhaps, though Marcia doesn't think of it in these terms.

4   When Marcia tells this story, it is almost identical but for two things: the intent and the ending. She says there was a parade that day moving below the window and I was too small to see over the balcony. I cried, waving my arms in the air. Marcia was watching the multi-coloured floats of tissue-paper flowers while hopping wildly from foot to foot to the rhythm of marching bands. She pointed and pointed but I was just too small. Then she had an idea (sometimes, she attributes this idea to one of the passing floats—the three bears sitting on small chairs or the elephant perched on its hind legs on a box). She went inside, dragged the piano stool to the balcony and lifted me onto it. Then she stood on it herself, and carefully hauled me over the railing. Here, the versions coincide, although Marcia always stresses the fact that she never let go of my ankles, in fact, was annoyed at my aunt for pulling me back before I could see the giant blue float with the yellow ducks on it. She's certain it was my aunt, and not my mother, of whom she has no recollection until years later. She always ends the story with, "The trouble with Mother is that she keeps trying to fit herself into other people's pasts," like a new character who shows up in a rewrite but who nobody recognizes.

5   When my aunt tells the story, she is lying on her bed in Italy, in a darkened room, shutters tight against the August heat, and I am reclined on a pink chaise lounge smoking Canadian cigarettes. She recalls the minutest details which imply that her story is the real one, or perhaps that she has the best imagination. For example, she says it was the 13th of August and she was wearing her black dress with the tiny blue flowers and the V-neck. We had all returned recently from our weekly visit to the cemetery where Marcia had thrown a tantrum when she wasn't allowed to pull all the petals off all the flowers. (My aunt had been widowed two years, she tells me.) In order to appease Marcia who was still crying, she took us upstairs to the balcony to watch the parade. After twenty minutes or so, she carried out the piano stool because her arms were aching from holding me up to the railing. She says Marcia was restless, thirsty; she had thrown her hat into the street and was now wailing and pointing at it as it wafted down.

6   My aunt gets up and goes to the kitchen, while I light another cigarette and push butts to one side of the ashtray. She returns with two glasses of orange juice and soda and lies back down on the bed. I have not seen her for twenty years and am anxious for her to fill the spaces in my memory, to confirm or deny, although why I should believe her versions, I don't know.

7   She says she only left the balcony for a few moments. She doesn't place blame or justify her actions, although she does tell me it was not easy looking after two little girls at her age.

8   The rest of the story coincides with Marcia's and this relieves me because two people surely couldn't invent the same details.

9   I don't recall the incident, although through hearing it, I've memorized the balcony and my position on it. I even imagine I can recall the people on the street at the time, although here logic fails me and when I retell the story, it is many years later and the balcony is on the 28th floor of a Vancouver apartment building. I am there with Harris, or Andrew, or some other English name. He is my lover of some weeks and it is his birthday. This story always occurs at night, downtown, when I can imagine the Vancouver skyline and the ships anchored in the harbour.

10   In the story, we've had a fabulous dinner—steak and lobster (flown in from the East Coast)—then Harris has blindfolded me (black silk scarf—implying ritual) to prepare me for a surprise. He leads me to the balcony door and slides it open. I feel the warm summer air and hear tires on wet pavement below although it is August and it hasn't rained for thirty-six days. Harris urges me over the sill onto the balcony, and walks behind me, his arms around my waist until a certain moment when he tells me to stop. Here, the details vary, according to my mood. Sometimes only his fingers touch my waist; other times I am leaning back against him and laughing. Either he removes the blindfold or I reach back and undo the knot. The moment I can see, however, the versions merge.

11   Harris has removed the balcony railing, and I am balanced precariously at the edge.

12   How long I stand there depends on the reaction of my audience. Then, Harris slowly pulls me back to the safety of the sliding glass door which feels solid even though I can see through it. I try to end the story here, by saying, "The trouble with me is that I'm too trusting," thereby absolving Marcia of all guilt, although she doesn't appear in this story.

13   More often than not, however, I am pestered into giving a denouement, when we all know some stories are best left at the climax. I vary these too. Sometimes I run out of the apartment forgetting my shoes and car keys and have to buzz Harris and go back up and retrieve them; other times I slap him across the face, square my shoulders and leave in a most dignified manner; other times I push him hard and he lands with his head over the edge of the abyss and begs for mercy. With this ending, I say, "The trouble with Harris is that he underestimates me," when actually it wasn't Harris at all, but my mother who keeps pushing me to the edge by restructuring my past until I'm unbalanced and can't trust my own memories.

14   When my father tells this story, he sets it in London, England (where he was at the time), on a foggy, grey day (probably to reconcile setting and content). He has just finished the first page of a letter to my aunt (my mother is with him), when he hears the cry of a child outside his window. He throws open the balcony doors in time to see a small girl holding a baby by its ankles over the railing of a balcony above. The girl is crying, "I can't hold her any more," and the baby is shrieking. Here, my father says he distinctly recognizes those voices as Marcia's and mine (even though he hadn't seen either of us since I was born). My father climbs the outside of his balcony railing, secures his feet into the rod ironwork and holds out his arms. Sometimes the balcony is concrete and he straddles it and has to lean into the street; other times it is wooden and rickety and he has to balance carefully to keep it from toppling. Often he is fully dressed because he is expecting an important visitor; occasionally he has just come out of the shower and is wearing only a towel. Below, a circle of people hold up the edges of a blanket or sometimes, the street is deserted. The ending, however, is always the same: the girl drops the baby which my father catches without incident. He ends this story with, "The trouble with children is that they have no concept of danger," which is true, considering how Marcia and I keep perching on the edge of a balcony, watching memories which shift dangerously from narrator to narrator and before I know it, I can't tell fact from fiction any more, and this is really dangerous because it implies that my life, the one I am trying to live so accurately, can and will be distorted, reordered, adjusted, and will emerge, years later, as a piece of fiction in some stranger's living room.

15   Now photographs. Yes, they tell a more precise story. Here's a family classic. In the middle of evergreens is a large tree with a thick branch on which my mother, Marcia and I are all standing. We are smiling, and wearing identical puffy dresses in pastels, with frilly crinolines underneath. My mother's mouth is especially beautiful; the crimson lipstick accentuates the whiteness of her teeth. Each of us is hugging the tree trunk or each other with one arm, and waving with the other to my father who is taking the picture. You have to look close to see that Marcia is wearing track shoes and she is standing on one of my mother's bare feet.

VOCABULARY

1. Find a word in paragraph 1 that means "to suddenly surprise someone."

_____

2. "In order to appease Marcia who was still crying, she took us upstairs to the balcony to watch the parade." (para. 5) Define *appease*.

_____

3. "She had thrown her hat into the street and was now wailing and pointing at it as it wafted down." (para. 5)

Guess the meaning of: *wailing*   _____

_____*wafted down* _____

4. Find a word in paragraph 13 that means "to annoy or bother someone."

_____

Guess which definition correctly defines the vocabulary word. It is a good idea to read the word in context before guessing. The paragraph number is in parentheses.

5. *hop* (4)
    a) a vine in the mulberry family
    b) to leap from one foot to the other
    c) to get aboard a moving vehicle

6. *straddle* (14)
    a) to spread the legs so that they are on the opposite sides of an object
    b) to walk with the legs wide apart
    c) to not take sides in an argument

7. *rickety* (14)
    a) a disease in the joints
    b) something that is unsound or shaky
    c) a drink containing lime juice

8. *topple* (14)
    a) to overthrow a leader
    b) to walk unsteadily
    c) to fall

READING COMPREHENSION

1. Genni Gunn describes several versions of the same story. The mother's version changes depending on the mother's mood, but the basic outline is as follows:

Mother's Version

Marcia holds baby over balcony and suspends her two storeys above street.

Mother tiptoes into room carefully (from street, or another room).

Mother grabs ankles of baby at the moment Marcia lets go.

Marcia's motive: jealousy.

How do Marcia's version, the aunt's version, and the father's version differ from the mother's version? (Refer to main events, and ignore details such as the clothing worn at the time.)

a) Write down Marcia's version: _____

_____

_____

_____

_____

What is Marcia's motive? _____

_____

b) Write down the aunt's version: _____

_____

_____

_____

_____

What is Marcia's motive in the aunt's story? _____

_____

c) Write down the father's version: _____

_____

_____

_____

_____

What is Marcia's motive in the father's story? _____

_____

2. The narrator describes her own version of the events to her friends. Is her version true? Why or why not?

_____

_____

_____

3. From the evidence, what do you think is the most truthful version of events? Support your answer with evidence from the text.

_____

_____

_____

4. What do you think Marcia's motive really was for holding her baby sister over the balcony railing? Support your answer with evidence from the text.

_____

_____

_____

5. Is the narrator still angry at Marcia or at her mother? Why?

_____

_____

_____

DISCUSSION

1. What methods can we use to judge which storyteller in "Versions" is most accurate?

2. We usually believe our own version of events, yet we can fool ourselves. The narrator in "Versions" states in paragraph 14 that her father hasn't seen her since her birth. She contradicts herself in paragraph 15. What is the contradiction? What does the contradiction tell us about the narrator's version?

3. Do you believe everything you read in history books? Why or why not?

4. Can you think of any historical event where the versions of the event differ, depending on who tells the story?

5. Do you think that a historical event _can_ be retold truthfully? Why or why not?

6. Do you keep a personal diary? Do you record events truthfully?

Speaking Tips

Questioning a Presenter

In order to arrive at the truth, we must be able to effectively question others. Remember to use the proper question form. Most of the time you must use the following word order.

Question Word	Auxiliary	Subject	Verb	Rest of the Sentence
		Word Order for Questions		
Why	did	the soldiers	leave	their guns on the battlefield?
How long	does	it	take	to become addicted to television?
Where	are	the troops	stationed?	
What	has	the President	done	to improve the situation?

The auxiliary verbs (do, does, did, was, have, etc.) don't have to go before the subject of your question if the answer could replace the question word in your sentence. For example:

Who directed *Star Wars*? George Lucas directed *Star Wars*.

The answer, George Lucas, replaces the question word "who" in the sentence.

SPEAKING TIPS EXERCISE

Genni Gunn is a Canadian writer. Ask questions about her. Write each question using the following words in parentheses. For example:

(Where, live) *Where does Genni Gunn live?*

1. (How long, live there)

2. (Where, born)

3. (How long, write "Versions")

4. (Who, greatest influence)

5. (How often, publish a book)

6. (When, first story published)

7. (Which story, favorite)

8. (How much, earn)

9. (How far, live from here)

10. (How, get inspired, for "Versions")

Writing Suggestion

Choose one of the following topics, and write an opinion essay. Remember to write an essay plan, and use transitional words and phrases to give the essay coherence.

1. History books are never truly objective.
2. Newspapers do not give objective accounts of events.

Speaking Suggestion

The teacher will remind you of a recent event (political, social or environmental). Tape (in a language lab, if possible) or write down what you remember about the event. Mention where you got your information.

Listen to some of the versions. Will these versions of the event be exactly the same?

Question both your teacher and other students in order to determine the most probable version of events.

12 Fate

The theory of predestination, which is the belief that every detail of our lives is preordained, is terrifyingly real for some people. If our lives are preordained, then free will is an illusion, and we act, like puppets on a string, according to the whims of the puppet master.

Award-winning Canadian author Hugh Garner raises some intriguing questions on the subject of fate in his short story, "The Premeditated Death of Samuel Glover."

Reading 12.1

The Premeditated Death of Samuel Glover

by Hugh Garner

1   It's been nothing but questions all day at the office. Every few minutes one of the other draftsmen would come over to my board and ask me about Sam's death. "What happened last night? Were you with him? Did it knock him down? Run over him? How'd he look? Was there much blood?"

2   They have no idea what it's like seeing a friend get killed like that, and having to answer all the questions by the police, the taxi company lawyer, and then by the fellows at work the next day. I'm going to tell it once more, the whole thing, and then I'm through.

3   Every night at five o'clock for the last seven or eight years Sam Glover and I have taken the elevator together, going home. Sam would buy his evening paper in the lobby, and then we'd walk up the street as far as Queen where we separated, Sam to take a westbound streetcar, and me to take one going east.

4   It got to be a habit, this three-block walk, and I enjoyed it because Sam was an interesting old fellow to talk to. He was a bachelor who lived with a married sister away out in the west end of town. From some of the things he told me on these short walks I learned that he was a believer in things like fate and premeditation. It was his favourite subject, and

sometimes he'd point to people who passed us on the street and say, "There goes a man hurrying to his fate," or "He wants to reach his rendez-vous, that one."

5   When I'd laugh, he'd say "You'll find out some day that it's no joke. I've seen it happen. Every man is predestined to meet his death at a time and place already chosen, my boy."

6   I'd laugh and shake my head.

7   It was about three years ago that Sam told me where he was going to die. We were waiting for the lights to change at the intersection of Adelaide Street, when Sam said, "This is the place where fate is going to catch up to me."

8   I looked down at him and laughed, thinking he was joking. He was the type of mousy little guy who would joke like that—or dismember a corpse.

9   "You may laugh, son, but it's true," he asserted in the good-natured, yet serious, way he had.

10   "Do you mean to tell me that you're going to be killed on this corner?" I asked.

11   "That's right," he answered soberly.

12   When the lights changed, we crossed the street. I said to Sam, "If you know that you're going to be killed here, why do you take this way home? You could walk a block east or west and take the streetcar from there."

13   "It wouldn't be much use trying to avoid it," he answered. "Some day I'd forget, or have some business to transact down here—"

14   "Well, suppose you decided not to die at all. You could move to another town and live forever."

15   "Nobody lives forever," he answered patiently. "You can't avoid your fate. This is where it will happen, and nothing I can do will prevent it. I'm just hoping that it won't be for some time yet." He looked up at me and smiled apologetically, but I could see that he meant every word.

16   After that I brought the subject up occasionally as we were crossing Adelaide Street, kidding him about being short-sighted, and about getting killed before his time if he wasn't careful. He would only smile at me and say, "You wait and see."

17   Last night we left the office as usual, about two minutes to five, in order to beat the rush to the elevators. Sam bought his paper in the lobby, and we went out into the street.

18   As we brushed through the five-o'clock crowd I asked Sam how his dyke drawings for the Mountview Refinery were coming along, and he told me he expected to finish them in a week; he was only waiting for some new tank specifications from McGuire, one of the engineers.

19   Looking up into the blue sky above the buildings I said, "It's going to be a nice evening. A change from the rain we've been having."

20   "Yes, it is. I'm going to do a little lawn bowling tonight," he answered. "It'll be my first chance this year. The greens have been a mess up to now."

21   When we reached the corner of Adelaide the lights were in our favour and we began to cross with the crowd. They changed from green to amber when we were half-way across, but we still had plenty of time. He stuck close to me as he always did. I saw this taxi cut around

the traffic and begin to cross the intersection as soon as it got the green light, so I shouted to Sam and ran the last few yards to the sidewalk.

22   I looked around and saw the taxi pick him up and throw him with a sickening plop against a hydrant about twenty feet from the corner. There was the scream of the taxi's brakes and a lot of yelling from the crowd.

23   By the time I got there two men had laid Sam out on the sidewalk. Everybody was crowding around to get a better look at him. He was dead, of course. One side of his head was squashed like the soft spot of an orange.

24   A policeman butted his way through the crowd and asked what had happened. The hack driver came over from his car and told the policeman that he hadn't had a chance, this old man ran right in front of his cab. He seemed to be a nice young fellow, and he wanted us all to believe him. I told the policeman I was a friend of Sam's, and that I'd seen the accident. I assured the driver that it wasn't his fault.

25   The taxi company lawyer came to my place later in the evening and questioned me about the accident. "I can't understand why he'd turn around and run the other way," he kept on saying.

26   "I've told you it wasn't your driver's fault, so why do you keep asking me questions like that?"

27   "O.K. I'm only trying to dope this thing out in case they have an inquest," he said.

28   If they have an inquest, I'm going to tell the truth. I've been thinking it over and I feel sure that Sam would have wanted it that way.

29   I had nothing against the old fellow, but after listening for so long to him bragging about knowing where he was going to die, it seemed I had to find out whether he was right or not. When I shouted at him to turn back, it wasn't me talking at all. Call it fate or predestination, or what you like, but that's what killed Sam Glover.

VOCABULARY

1. Read paragraphs 10 and 11, and circle the best definition for the word *soberly*.
   a) not affected by passion or prejudice
   b) the opposite of "drunk"
   c) a serious or grave mood

2. Find a word in paragraph 16 that means "to tease."

_____

3. Find a word in paragraph 18 that means "a bank of earth to hold back water."

_____

4. What is a *hack driver*? (para. 24)

_____

_____

5. Define *dope* as it is used in paragraph 27.

_____

_____

6. Define *bragging*. (para. 29)

_____

_____

READING COMPREHENSION

1. Did the cab driver break the law by going through a red light? _____

2. When Sam and the narrator were crossing the intersection at the time of the accident, what colour was the light when they began crossing?

_____

3. When the narrator saw the cab coming, in which direction did he run?

_____

4. As the cab came towards the two men, what did the narrator shout to Sam?

_____

5. Why did the narrator shout those words?

_____

_____

6. In the conclusion (para. 29), the narrator says, "after listening for so long to him bragging..." What does his use of the word *bragging* tell you about the narrator's feelings towards Sam?

_____

_____

_____

7. Does the narrator believe in predestination? Support your answer.

_____

_____

8. What is the main idea of the story? (Ask yourself the "who, what, when, where, how and why" questions)

_____

_____

_____

DISCUSSION

1. Who or what is responsible for Sam's death?

2. Is Sam responsible for his own death?

3. Do you believe in destiny? Why or why not?

4. If it were true that everyone "is predestined to meet his (or her) death at a time and place already chosen" (para. 5), would you want to know when, where or how you'll die?

Speaking Tips
Oral Opinion Presentations

There are a few points to remember when you make an oral presentation.

Structure Your Presentation
Your oral presentations should be clearly structured. You should have an introduction, main points and a conclusion that brings your presentation to a satisfactory closing. More information about structuring an oral opinion assignment can be found in Chapter 3 in the Writing Tips section.

Don't Read
When you come to class, be prepared to speak to the audience. Do not read your presentation, as it is very boring for the audience.

Use Cue Cards

Prepare your assignment in advance. You should make an outline. Then, on your cue cards, you should write down main words for your introduction, your arguments and your conclusion.

Do not write down every word of your text on the cue cards. You only refer to your cue cards to remind you of your points. If your entire text is written on the cards, you will need to hunt for information which will distract your audience. You should not have any breaks in the flow of your presentation. For example:

The First Point in Your Argument:

With their huge salaries, movie actors live decadent lives in a time when most people in North America are struggling to make ends meet. A slouching New York actor has a limo follow him on his walks through town in case he gets tired. A famous actress bought a Victorian mansion just to have a place to keep her huge doll collection! A well known young actor buys new clothing in every city he visits rather than bother with luggage. The overly large salaries just turn these actors into spoiled brats.

Cue Card

> 1st point
> Actors – decadent lives / most struggle
> – slouching actor limo on walks
> – Actress mansion for her dolls
> – Young actor no luggage – buys new clothes
> Actors = spoiled brats

Rehearse

Rehearse your presentation! Do not expect to ad-lib a formal presentation of opinion, as the odds of you forgetting something important are rather high. Also, your teacher will not be impressed if you must frequently pause to think of something to say.

Credit Your Sources

If you paraphrase or quote someone, or borrow an argument that you read somewhere else, give credit to your source. Whenever you use someone else's words, it is essential that you mention the name of the article, and the author's name.

Writing Suggestion

Write an essay about one of these topics.

1. I know someone who "saw" the future. (This essay could be in the narrative, or story-telling form.)

2. Why do religions exist?

3. There is no such thing as predestination.

Speaking Suggestion

In groups, predict future events. Predict two political, two social, two environmental and two sports events. Record your predictions and share them with class members.

The Present Tenses

Simple Present (General Present)

The Simple Present tense is the first verb tense that most students learn, but it is also, perhaps, the most complicated, for in this tense the student must remember to pronounce and write the final *s* on verbs that refer to third person singular subjects. What further complicates this tense is the importance of adding the auxiliaries *do* or *does* when forming some questions or negatives. If you have ever found yourself forgetting the *s* on verbs, or omitting the *do* or *does*, then study this section with particular care.

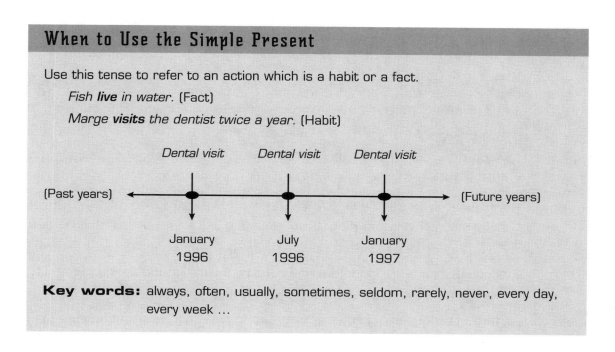

When to Use the Simple Present

Use this tense to refer to an action which is a habit or a fact.

*Fish **live** in water.* (Fact)

*Marge **visits** the dentist twice a year.* (Habit)

	Dental visit	Dental visit	Dental visit	
(Past years)	January 1996	July 1996	January 1997	(Future years)

Key words: always, often, usually, sometimes, seldom, rarely, never, every day, every week ...

Subject-Verb Agreement

I
We
You
They

> **live** in Manitoba.

He
She
It

> **lives** in Manitoba.

1. All simple present tense verbs that refer to *one* person, place or thing (except *you* and *I*) must be conjugated with an *s* or *es*.

Roy despis**es** coffee, but his wife, Ginger, lov**es** it.

2. Add *es* to verbs ending in *ch, sh, s, x,* or *z*.

Ginger search**es** for new types of coffee, and she sometimes mix**es** brands together.

3. Don't let interrupting phrases fool you.

That **house**, where John and Anne live, **has** many rooms.

The new **bicycle**, which is in pieces, **includes** a set of directions.

4. *Everybody, somebody, anybody* and *nobody* are considered singular. (Also with "everyone," "everything," etc.)

Somebody **has** my keys. Everyone **is** here. Something **is** under the rug.

5. Never add *s* to modals: *can, could, would, should, must, may, might, will, shall, ought to.*

Sara **can come** with us but Margie **must do** her homework.

CLASS EXERCISE

Underline each subject and circle each verb (action word). Add *s* or *es* to verbs that follow 3rd person singular subjects. Only the verb *to be* is already conjugated correctly. There are 20 verbs to conjugate in this text, not including the example.

(1) My neighbor, who is very friendly, (have) [has] a little mutt called Sparky. As you may have guessed from the name, Sparky is one of those annoying miniature dogs. Everyone say that Sparky look like an overgrown dustbunny. He have a tiny brown mop of fur for a head, and his body, which measure about eight inches in length, look like a furry black and brown boot.

(2) Sparky is a very jumpy, nervous little dog. I'd swear that he have a cup of cappuccino every morning. Every time that little mutt catch a glimpse of me he yap, leap, shiver, shake, and, if possible, bite. If I walk on the sidewalk in front of the neighbor's house, Sparky inevitably come racing around the corner at full tilt. This is such a dumb dog that sometimes he run right past me, look momentarily confused, turn in a skid, and charge back at me. He bark, jump up and he grab my pant leg. He is more annoying than a flea on a dog's neck.

EXERCISE 1

Complete this exercise in the same way as you did the exercise above. Conjugate 20 verbs in this text. The verb *to be* is already conjugated.

Note: *to go, to eat,* etc. are infinitives. Never add *s* to the verb that follows *to*.

(1) Ms. Murti is a very friendly woman. She have a very gentle disposition and she seem to really care about others. One of the things that everyone notice about her is the *intensity* with which she listen. When anyone talk to her, she always immediately stop whatever she is doing, she turn, and look the speaker in the eye. This ability to really listen is a quality that I admire. Ms. Murti, with her listening ability, manage to make you feel like you are the most important person in the world.

(2) Mr. Murti is not at all like his wife. He have a very gruff manner. When someone address him, he often look away, as if he can't hear that person. Everyone notice how impolite he is. Mr. Murti also interrupt people, and when he have an opinion about something, he make sure that everyone know about it. Mr. Murti, who usually ignore or insult people, actually think that he is a very pleasant fellow! Most people like Ms. Murti more than Mr. Murti.

Simple Present Tense: Negative Form

With the verb *to be*, just put *not* after the verb.

Carol is friendly. *Carol **is not** friendly. (or **isn't**)*

With all other verbs, place *do* or *does* and the word *not* between the subject and the verb.

Aldo and I watch a lot of TV. *We **do not** watch a lot of TV. (or **don't**)*

Mrs. Murti listens carefully. *She **does not** listen carefully. (or **doesn't**)*

EXERCISE 2

Underline the verb and make it negative.

Example: The doctor <u>has</u> a nice bedside manner. _doesn't have_____

1. Ronald remembers every detail about his childhood. _____

2. Carlos eats fried food. _____

3. Those workers go on strike every year. _____

4. Tomatoes are very tasty. _____

5. April has 31 days. _____

Simple Present Tense: Question Form

The verb *to be*: When making a question, change the word order so that *be* appears *before* the subject.

Diego (is) thirsty.   (Is) Diego thirsty?

                            Why **is** Diego thirsty?

With all other verbs, add the auxiliary *do* or *does* to create questions. When you add *does* to the sentence, the *s* is no longer needed on the verb.

                                                    auxiliary
Rebeka stretches every morning.   When   **does**   Rebeka   **stretch?**
Jerome walks in his sleep.   How often **does** Jerome   **walk** in his sleep?

EXERCISE 3

Create questions from the answers provided.

		Question word(s)	Auxiliary	Subject	Verb	
	Example: Jerry hates dogs.	Why	does	Jerry	hate	dogs?
1.	Hanna needs a lift.	What				
2.	The peas are on the plate.	Where				
3.	The twins usually play hockey.	When				
4.	Marco often lies to people.	Why				
5.	The police investigate themselves.	Why				
6.	The doctor is late today.	Why				
7.	The movie lasts for two hours.	How long				

Who / What Questions

When *who(m)** and *what* ask about the object of a question, an auxiliary is necessary.

The roof needs **new shingles**.   **What does** the roof need?

Tony phones **his mother** every day.   **Who** (or **whom**) **does** Tony call every day?

*Whom is rarely used in spoken English.

However, when *who* and *what* ask about the subject of a question, no auxiliary is needed.

The roof needs new shingles.   **What** needs new shingles?

Tony phones his mother every day.   **Who** phones his mother every day?

EXERCISE 4

Write questions. The answer to the question is in bold.

Example:

The boy has **peanuts** in his pocket.   _What does the boy have in his pocket?_

1. The nurse has **a clipboard**.   _____
2. **The nurse** has a clipboard.   _____
3. **Samantha** wears second-hand clothes.   _____
4. Samantha wears **second-hand clothes**.   _____
5. **That house** has a large garage.   _____

EXERCISE 5

Write questions. The answer to the question is in bold.

1. **Frankie** has a lot of problems at school.

   _____

2. Sparky lives **in my neighbor's house**.

   _____

3. Coffee gives many people **the jitters**.

   _____

4. The ballet performance lasts **for two and a half hours**.

   _____

5. Ms. Riffo visits the dentist **twice a year**.

   _____

6. The skunks hide **under the shed** every spring.

   _____

7. Chuck opens beer bottles **with his teeth**.

   _____

Make the next three questions *negative*. With negative questions, attach *not* to the auxiliary.

She doesn't own a television.   _Why **doesn't** she **own** a television?_

Mark isn't home.   _Why **isn't** he home?_

8. Francis and Charles aren't friendly to each other. (Why?)

   _____

9. That car doesn't have any wheels. (Why?)

   _____

10. Mark has no friends. (Why? Rephrase question to make a negative question.)

    _____

Present Progressive

The Present Progressive is used whenever you want to indicate that an action is in progress. This tense is formed with a present form of *be*, and *ing* is added to the verb. For example, at this moment I am writing this sentence. I could not say *At this moment I write this sentence*. Sometimes students forget to add *be* before the verb (*I writing*), but it is important to form this tense correctly.

Another problem area with this tense is the correct spelling of the *ing* verb form. Should you double the last letter (*omitting*) or not (*opening*)? The rules for spelling are explained in this section.

As you know, for most rules there are exceptions. In this tense, there are certain verbs that cannot be used in the progressive form even if the action is happening now. For example, you cannot say *I am believing you now*. With the verb *believe* you must use the simple present tense even if you are talking about this moment: *I believe you now*. These *non-progressive* verbs are listed in this section, and you should remember that these verbs are non-progressive (never used in an *ing* form) in *all* progressive tenses.

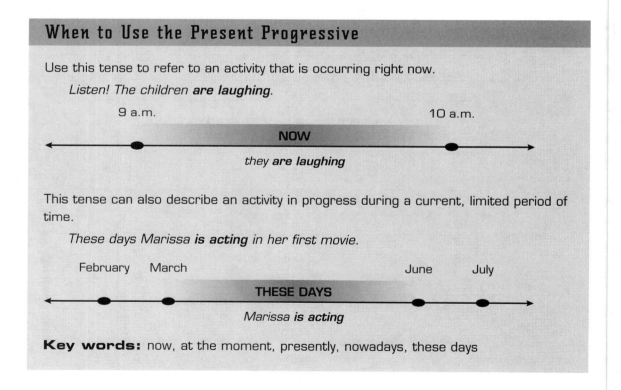

When to Use the Present Progressive

Use this tense to refer to an activity that is occurring right now.

*Listen! The children **are laughing**.*

9 a.m. — NOW — 10 a.m.

they **are laughing**

This tense can also describe an activity in progress during a current, limited period of time.

*These days Marissa **is acting** in her first movie.*

February March — THESE DAYS — June July

Marissa **is acting**

Key words: now, at the moment, presently, nowadays, these days

Present Progressive Tense: Question Form

Be acts as an auxiliary and goes before the subject.

Rick (is) climbing a ladder.   *Why (is) Rick climbing a ladder?*

Present Progressive Tense: Negative Form

Place *not* after the verb *be*.

Alf is studying for his test.   Alf **is not (isn't)** studying for his test.

CLASS EXERCISE

Make *a statement, a question,* and *a negative sentence* out of the words in parentheses. Use either the simple present or the present progressive tense.

Example: (Carol / bite her lip / now)   *She's biting her lip now.*
                                          Is she biting her lip now?
                                          She isn't biting her lip now.

1. (the politician / lie / everyday) _____

_____

_____

2. (your sister / cut her toenails / now) _____

_____

_____

3. (Mr. Ed / have / long dirty hair) _____

_____

_____

4. (Terri / knock / on the door) _____

_____

_____

5. (your brother / have a temper tantrum / now) _____

_____

_____

6. (most people / have / a television) _____

_____

_____

7. (you / need a passport / to visit Mexico) _____

_____

_____

8. (the children / understand / Spanish) _____

_____

_____

Non-Progressive Verbs

These verbs cannot be used in the progressive tense.

Perception verbs	Preference verbs	State verbs
see	like	know
hear	love	think (opinion)
feel	hate	mean
taste	care	suppose
smell	prefer	understand
appear	want	believe
look (meaning "appear")	wish	realize
seem	desire	own / belong

Some of these verbs can be used in the present progressive tense when they describe a process or action.

Compare:

I am looking at you.   *That dinner looks good!*

He is seeing Rosa. (meaning: dating)   *Louis sees really well without glasses.*

EXERCISE 6

Complete the sentences using the simple present or the present progressive. Use the Present Progressive (*be ...ing*) when the action is in progress now, or for this period of time.

1. I (know) _____ Ziggy Brown. (you, know) _____ him? He (act, sometimes) _____ in the theater with my brother. I (think) _____ they (rehearse) _____ for a show right now.

2. This tea (smell) _____ good. I (like) _____ strong tea, but my husband, Ed, (drink, not) _____ it. He (think) _____ that caffeine gives him the jitters. Now he (relax) _____ in front of the TV set. He (watch) _____ a football game. Sometimes Ed (act) _____ like a real couch potato. I (like, not) _____ to watch TV.

3. At the moment my brother (live) _____ in Toronto. He (look) _____ for a job anywhere in Canada. My parents were born in Calgary and they (live, still) _____ in Alberta. My younger sister (stay) _____ with my parents temporarily until she gets accepted at a university. She (wait) _____ for news from one of Canada's universities. As for me, I (live) _____ in Halifax. I am a computer programmer, but I (work, not) _____ right now.

Spelling of ing *Verb Forms*

1. When verbs end in *y*, always keep the *y* and add *ing*.

try – *trying*   play – *playing*

2. Double the *last* letter of one-syllable verbs that end with a consonant-vowel-consonant combination.

run – *running*   stop – *stopping*

Exceptions: *Quit* (two vowels) becomes **quit**t*ing*.

3. Double the last letter of longer verbs when they end in a *stressed* consonant-vowel-consonant combination.

re**fer** – *referring*   **o**pen – *opening*
(Second syllable is stressed,   (First syllable is stressed,
so double the last letter.)   so do not double the last letter.)

Exceptions: Never double the last letter of verbs ending in *w* or *x*.

EXERCISE 7

Write the present participle (*ing* form) in the space provided.

1. come _____   **6.** happen _____

2. open _____   **7.** occur _____

3. tip _____   **8.** rain _____

4. shop _____   **9.** remain _____

5. write _____   **10.** omit _____

CLASS EXERCISE

Fill in the blanks with the simple present tense or the present progressive tense.

1. What (happen) _____ these days? I (refer) _____
to the violence in the world. Humans (kill) _____ each other, at
this moment, in every country on the planet.

2. Alice (sit, usually) _____ in the back row of movie theaters but
today she (sit) _____ in the front row. She (wear, not)
_____ her glasses today, so she (see, not) _____
well. Today I (sit, also) _____ near the front.

3. At the moment Kevin (stare) _____ out his window. The
children (shout) _____ and some trucks (honk)

_____ their horns. A thief (rob) _____
the corner store. The store's alarm system (wail) _____ .
I (hear, not) _____ any traffic and I (smell, not)
_____ any pollution because I live in the countryside.

4. Clara (knit) _____ a sweater for her son. Many people
(know, not) _____ how to knit. (your father,
know) _____ how to knit?

5. Karen (date) _____ someone these days. I (know)
_____ it! Look at her over there! She (walk)
_____ around like she is on cloud nine. Hey! (you, listen)
_____ to me right now?

When to Use Apostrophes

Use apostrophes:

1. to join a subject and verb together.   *We're late. **There's** nothing to eat.*

2. to join an auxiliary with *not*.   *I **can't** come. They **aren't** very friendly.*

3. to indicate possession.   *That is **Simon's** car. **Ross's** computer is new.*

Never use an apostrophe before the **s** at the end of a verb.

   Incorrect: *Mother make's*

   Correct: *Mother makes*

EXERCISE 8

Add apostrophes where necessary.

1. Hannas father, Fred, works for General Motors, but Freds taking a vacation right now.

2. The Maliks live near the mines, but the Girards home is near the lake.

3. Mr. Maliks son needs work now, but he doesnt want to work in the mines.

4. He wants to work at his uncles company, but right now there arent any jobs available.

5. Mr. Girards daughter works at Smiths Appliances, but she doesnt want to stay there.

EXERCISE 9

Underline and correct the errors in the following present tense sentences. If the sentence is correct, write *C* in the space provided.

1. Nobody deserve to suffer through a long and painful illness. _____

2. Barney is very athletic and he is going to the gym every second day. _____

3. Alice and Dan eats dinner together every Friday night. _____

4. Simon isn't understanding you very well, so please speak more slowly. _____

5. Melanie, who work's with me, is very ill right now. _____

6. Why is Clara is sitting all alone over there? _____

7. The children are so quiet! I think they are relaxing in the back yard. _____

8. Sorry, but Mary is a person who don't like to eat meat. _____

9. Do anybody want more coffee? _____

10. Laura is the type of person who always judge a book by its cover. _____

CLASS EXERCISE

The present tense verbs in this text are in *italics*. Some of the verbs are spelled and used correctly, but others have errors. Correct any verb errors. After the example, there are 12 errors.

(1) Right now I ⟨*siting*⟩ on my back porch, and I *am watching* an amazing event that *is occuring* before my eyes. The mountains, which *form's* a wall on the horizon, *stand* majestically, and the clouds *are* in the shape of an arch. All of the clouds above the arch *are* thick and gray, and the sky inside the arch *is* clear blue. The chinook winds *are comming* with their warm, balmy air and I *am enjoying* every minute of it.

(2) Although I left this town many years ago, I *am* extremely happy to be back. The big sky *is* something that a prairie person never *forget*. Anyone who *live* near here *know* what I'm talking about. The flat, golden prairies *stretches* for miles, and the sky *seems* infinite in its grandeur. Occasionally, at a moment when everyone *are busy walking, working, writting letters, and basically living* an ordinary existence, the sky suddenly *lights* up with flashes of color that *seems* to reflect from the earth. The northern lights *are* breathtaking, the chinook arches *are* glorious, and even the clear blue sky *attract* people's attention. Here, on the edge of the prairies, everyone always *study* the sky.

Present Tenses in the Passive Voice

A sentence is *active* when the subject of the sentence does the action, and *passive* when the subject of the sentence receives the action. Passive voice should not be overused, and is effective mainly when the result of the action is more important than who performed the action.

1. In the *simple present* tense, the passive voice is formed with *be* (am / is / are) + the past participle. (See the verb list at the end of this book.)

Active	Passive
*Many students **use** computers.*	*Computers **are used** by many students.*
Students do the action.	The subject (*computers*) is acted on by the students.

2. In the *present progressive* tense, the passive voice is formed with the present progressive form of *be* (am being / is being / are being) + the past participle.

Active	Passive
*Right now Julie **is using** the printer.*	*The printer **is being used**. (by Julie)**

*The "*by* ... " phrase is not always necessary.

EXERCISE 10

Change the following sentences from the active to the passive voice. The verb to be changed is in italics.

> Example: My son *is washing* the kitchen floor.
>
> *The kitchen floor is being washed by my son.*

1. General Motors *produces* many cars.

_____

2. As we speak, the workers *are producing* over forty cars.

_____

3. Right now the B team *is making* a car door.

_____

4. People in this area also *create* many other products.

_____

5. People on assembly lines *manufacture* many useful products.

_____

6. Unfortunately, machines *are replacing* human workers these days.

_____

2 The Past Tenses

The past tenses in English do not contain complexities like *s* on third person singular verbs. Only the verb *be* has two past forms (*was* and *were*). In fact, in some respects the past tense is relatively simple: the same verb form (such as *looked*) can be used with all persons.

However, this tense is complicated because of the irregular verb forms that must be memorized. There is a list of common irregular past tense verbs at the back of this book. The Simple Past, like the Simple Present, also requires an auxiliary (*did*) in most question and negative forms.

Simple Past

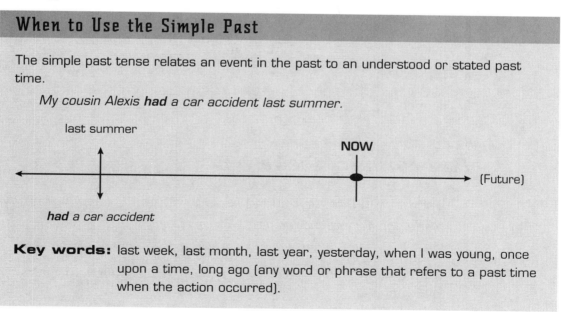

When to Use the Simple Past

The simple past tense relates an event in the past to an understood or stated past time.

*My cousin Alexis **had** a car accident last summer.*

last summer

NOW

(Future)

had a car accident

Key words: last week, last month, last year, yesterday, when I was young, once upon a time, long ago (any word or phrase that refers to a past time when the action occurred).

Spelling of Regular Past Tense Verbs

There are both regular and irregular past tense verbs. Regular verbs take *ed* and generally do not appear in verb lists, such as the one at the back of this book, because of their standard form.

1a. Double the *last* letter of one-syllable verbs that end in a consonant-vowel-consonant combination.

stop – *stopped*   jog – *jogged*

1b. Double the last letter of longer verbs when they end in a *stressed* consonant-vowel-consonant combination.

pre**fer** – *preferred*   **o**pen – *opened*
(Second syllable is stressed,   (First syllable is stressed,
so double the last letter)   so do not double the last letter)

2a. When verbs end in consonant-*y*, change the *y* to *i* and add *ed*.

fry – *fried*   apply – *applied*

2b. When verbs end in vowel-*y*, usually keep the *y*.

play – *played*   **Exception:** pay – *paid*

EXERCISE 1

Write the *ed* form of these regular verbs.

1. believe _____   **6.** remain _____   **11.** rain _____

2. prefer _____   **7.** jog _____   **12.** try _____

3. rely _____   **8.** offer _____   **13.** plan _____

4. marry _____   **9.** hope _____   **14.** die _____

5. happen _____   **10.** tip _____   **15.** open _____

Past Forms of the Verb Be

1. Use *was* with *I*, *he*, *she* and *it*. Use *were* with *you*, *we* and *they*.

Marla, the girl with the red hair, **was** very flighty.

Patrick and Alice were late for class yesterday.

2. With "dummy" subjects like *there*, make sure that your verb agrees with the following nouns.

There **was** a tiny ink **stain** on my sweater.

There **were** several ink **stains** on his sleeve.

EXERCISE 2

Fill in the blanks with the simple past verb forms.

1. When I (be) _____ a child, I (visit) _____ my grandmother every summer. Granny Maud (have) _____ the unusual habit of frequently moving, so whenever we (look) _____ for her home, we had to get the new address from one of my uncles.

2. Although Granny (move) _____ often, she was very consistent in one way: her homes always (contain) _____ a special glassed-off room. This salon, where the plastic-covered furniture (be) _____ kept, (be) _____ always off-limits to the grandchildren.

3. As children we often (press) _____ our noses against the glass to look at the fancy furniture in the salon. There (be) _____ always many statues, elaborately framed photos and unusual knickknacks. One of the items that I especially (enjoy) _____ (be) _____ a tiny porcelain clock. Inside the decorated clock (be) _____ two tiny girls sitting on a tiny swing. As each second (tick) _____ the tiny girls swung like a pendulum.

4. Unfortunately I rarely (try) _____ to tell my granny how much I loved her. The day that my granny (stop) _____ breathing, it (occur) _____ to me that I really (miss) _____ her.

Irregular Verbs

EXERCISE 3

Do you know the past forms of these irregular verbs? Write the past tense form in the space provided.

1. keep _____	**6.** sink _____	**11.** sleep _____
2. write _____	**7.** think _____	**12.** buy _____
3. bring _____	**8.** feel _____	**13.** ring _____
4. fall _____	**9.** sell _____	**14.** hang _____
5. spend _____	**10.** fight _____	**15.** shake _____

Past Tense: Question Form

Verb Be

When making a question, change the word order so that the verb *be* appears before the subject.

They (were) late.   (Were) they late?

Why **were** they late?

All Other Verbs

With all other verbs, add the auxiliary *did* to create questions. When you add *did* to the sentence, you no longer need to keep the verb in the past tense. *Did* makes the question a past tense question.

<table>
<tr><td></td><td>auxiliary</td><td></td></tr>
<tr><td>Ralph married Alice in 1958.</td><td>When</td><td>**did**</td><td>Ralph **marry** Alice?</td></tr>
<tr><td>Marvin drank too much beer.</td><td>Why</td><td>**did**</td><td>Marvin **drink** all of the beer?</td></tr>
</table>

When *who* or *what* ask about the *subject* of a question, no *did* is required.

Who drank too much beer?   Marvin drank too much beer.

Past Tense: Negative Form

Verb Be

Place *not* after the verb *be*.

They were **not** late.

All Other Verbs

Place *not* after the auxiliary.

Ralph **did not** marry Alice in 1958.

EXERCISE 4

Make questions from the following sentences. The answer is in bold.

Example: Becky ate **the grapes**.   *What did Becky eat?*

1. Marco called **Alicia** yesterday.

_____

2. **Marco** called Alicia yesterday.

_____

3. Sam cut her toenails **because they were too long**.

_____

4. Ricardo and Mia sang **"La Bamba"** at the festival.

_____

5. Mia sang in a choir **for twelve years**.

_____

6. Robert did the laundry **last Saturday**.

_____

7. Ricky went to a hockey game **yesterday**.

_____

8. The farm was **four kilometers** from the nearest phone.

_____

9. Her dead dog's name was **Lucky**.

_____

10. Moe gave the bookie **fifty dollars** yesterday.

_____

11. Denis made **blueberry muffins** last weekend.

_____

12. Bert swam **across the lake** last summer.

_____

EXERCISE 5

In the following sentences, underline the verb(s) and change them to the past tense.

	Now	**In 1974**
	Example: Maurice <u>keeps</u> his valuables in a safe.	_kept_
1.	Mrs. Romanov teaches children how to speak Russian.	_____
2.	Anton chooses to learn German also.	_____
3.	Anton writes, but doesn't speak, German.	_____
4.	Anton's sister Katya flies a single-engine plane.	_____
5.	Anton doesn't know how to fly a plane.	_____
6.	Katya spends a lot of time in the air.	_____
7.	Mrs. Romanov shakes when she goes into an airplane.	_____
8.	She is afraid of heights.	_____
9.	Katya pays for her own flying lessons.	_____
10.	By paying for her lessons, Katya proves that she is independent.	_____

When Not *to Use the Past Verb Form*

Never use the past verb form:

1. after *to* in infinitive forms.

    Incorrect: *The children needed to spoke with us.*

    Correct: *The children needed **to speak** with us.*

2. after *did. Did* makes a sentence past tense, and the following verb must be in the present form.

    Incorrect: *Mother didn't told us why you were late.*

    Correct: *Mother **didn't tell** us why you were late.*

CLASS EXERCISE

Correct the verb errors in the following sentences. There is one error per sentence.

1. Last weekend I really wanted to saw that rock band, but the tickets were too expensive.

2. When I was a child, there was rules, and we had to follow them.

3. The insects didn't survived the pesticide spraying.

4. My teacher, Ms. Ritchie, tought me how to play the piano.

5. A long time ago a king made a tournament to knew who would get the throne.

6. Tweetie Bird tought he saw a putty cat a moment ago.

7. Did he saw a cat?

8. What happened when the fight was over?

9. There was over forty people at the wedding reception.

10. The legendary King Arthur wanted to found a queen.

Avoiding Tense Shifts

If you start to tell a story, do not shift tenses unless the time frame really does change.

    *Jerry **left** his apartment and Kramer **enters** moments later.*

    (The tense incorrectly shifts from the past to the present.)

EXERCISE 6

In the following exercise, correct any tense shifts. In the past tense, use *would* instead of *will*.

(1) Some people really want to be alone and preferred to spend most of their time in solitary activities. Joan, a girl that I went to school with, was really like that. Every day when we went outside for recess, Joan stays inside. When the other kids played with skipping ropes and marbles, Joan will sit quietly in a corner of the schoolyard and read a book. Sometimes I asked Joan to play with us but she never wants to.

(2) Even though she didn't have any friends at school, she never seems lonely. She will smile to herself as she did her solitary activities. I met Joan many years later, when I was about nineteen, on an airplane. She told me that she was going to France to study mime. She seemed so friendly and happy. We sat together on the flight and talk for hours.

Past Progressive

The Past Progressive is formed with the past forms of the verb *be* (*was, were*) and the *ing* verb form. This tense is sometimes overused by second language learners. For example, French speakers sometimes incorrectly translate the *imparfait* into the past progressive. Only use the past progressive tense when you want to specify that one action was in progress when another action occurred, or when you want to indicate that a past action was in progress at a specific past time.

For example, it is incorrect to say *Yesterday I was watching TV.* Unless you spent the entire day in front of the television, such a sentence doesn't make sense. It would be more appropriate in this case to use the simple past, and say *Yesterday I watched TV.* Now the sentence just means that at some point yesterday you watched TV, but you probably did many other things as well.

Only use the past progressive in the following two ways. You could say *Yesterday at noon I was watching TV.* In this sentence you clarify that the past action was in progress at a specific time. You could also say *Yesterday while I was watching TV the power went out*, indicating that the past action was in progress when another action occurred.

Keep in mind that some verbs are non-progressive, and the list in Chapter 1 also applies to past progressive verbs. For example, you cannot say *I was understanding* because *understand* cannot be used in the progressive form.

When to Use the Past Progressive

Use the past progressive to:

1. describe an action that was in progress when another action interrupted it.

*Last Friday we **were watching** TV when Anne fainted.*

we ***were watching*** *TV*   **NOW**

←——————————————————————————————————→

Interruption: Anne fainted

2. describe an action that was in progress at a specific, indicated time.

*Yesterday evening at 8 p.m. I **was eating** supper.*

*I **was eating** supper*   **NOW**

←——————————————————————————————————→

Precise time: 8 p.m.

3. describe two actions that were continuing at the same time.

Yesterday, while I **was setting** the table, my sister **was resting** on the sofa.*
*Use the past progressive after *while*.

EXERCISE 7

Fill in the blanks with the simple past or the past progressive tense.

1. During my childhood, I (understand, not) _____ the value of education.

2. Yesterday evening, Steve (read) _____ a book in the bathroom when I (yell) _____ that supper was ready.

3. The students (discuss) _____ the issue when Evan suddenly (faint) _____ . In the past, my old teacher often (discuss) _____ that issue.

4. The bride (walk) _____ up the aisle when she (slip) _____ on a banana peel. (You, see) _____ the bride slip on the banana peel? It was very funny!

5. I really had to complain to the landlord. Last night, while I (try) _____ to sleep, my downstairs neighbour (play) _____ his saxophone!

6. On March 1, at the time of the murder, I (babysit) _____ my sister's children in the park. I (see, not) _____ or (hear) _____ a thing.

CLASS EXERCISE

Put either the simple past or the past progressive verb form in the spaces provided. (20 spaces)

1. My grandfather (come) _____ to Canada in 1924. He (leave) _____ Russia, and he (ride) _____ across Europe on the railroad. His family then (board) _____ a ship headed to America. They (have) _____ almost no possessions, but my grandfather had a gold wristwatch that his uncle had given him.

2. As the boat (leave) _____ France, my grandfather (lean) _____ on the rail to watch the receding shore. While he (bend) _____ over to look at the water, the gold watch (slip) _____ from his wrist and (fall) _____ into the ocean.

3. While the ship (cross) _____ the ocean, my grandfather (fall) _____ ill. He (have) _____ a fever, and his parents (be, not) _____ sure that my grandfather would survive. For several hours he (lose) _____ consciousness. A large storm (hit) _____ while the boat (approach) _____ the Canadian shore. While the ship (toss) _____ and (turn) _____ on the waves, my grandfather (regain) _____ consciousness.

Past Tenses in the Passive Voice

The past tense, like the present tense, has a passive voice form.

1. In the simple past, the passive voice is formed with the past form of *be* (was / were) + the past participle.

Active

Workers from China **made** *that coat.*

Passive

That coat **was made** *in China. (by workers)*

2. In the past progressive, the passive voice is formed with the past progressive form of *be* (was being / were being) + the past participle.

Active

At 8 p.m., John **was using** *the machine.*

Passive

At 8 p.m., the machine **was being used**. *(by John)*

EXERCISE 8

Determine if the following sentences are active or passive. Underline the verb and write *P* (Passive) or *A* (Active) in the space provided.

1. Boots are sold at that store.   _____

2. I bought a nice pair of leather boots there last Tuesday.   _____

3. The boots were made in Mexico.   _____

4. Now I am wearing the boots.   _____

5. At work I was asked about the boots.   _____

CLASS EXERCISE

Fill in the blanks with the past tense form in either the active or the passive voice.

1. A few years ago a great chess-playing computer (develop) _____ by an American company. The chess champion, Gary Kasparov, (challenge) _____ to a match by the computer company. The company (want) _____ to see if their computer, "Deep Blue," could beat a human opponent.

2. Just before his fortieth move, Kasparov (pick) _____ up his watch and (put) _____ it on. A ripple of laughter (hear) _____ from the crowd. The "watch" manoeuvre (mean) _____ that Kasparov (feel) _____ confident that the game was his.

3. Many people (surprise) _____ by the strong performance of the computer, but they (feel) _____ relieved that humanity's superiority over machines was still intact. After winning the game, Kasparov (give) _____ a standing ovation by the crowd.

The Present Perfect Tenses

What can complicate second-language learning is the fact that some languages have tenses that don't exist in other languages. For example, English has a tense called the Present Perfect, but no such tense exists in French.

If you listen to English people speak, you will notice that this tense is very common, and is used in many circumstances. For example, the following paragraph is one side of a typical telephone call. Can you identify the present perfect tense in this example?

> I haven't seen you for a while. Have you done anything interesting lately? Have you seen any good movies? Have you gone to any good plays? I haven't been out of the house for two weeks, because I've had a terrible cold. On top of that, my sister has been in town for the last week, and she hasn't had time to see me yet.

This tense is always formed with an auxiliary (*have* or *has*) and the past participle. You can never use the simple past verb form with this tense. For example, you cannot say *I have already ate*. You must use the past participle *eaten* in order to form the correct sentence, *I have already eaten*. A list of irregular past participles is at the back of this book.

In order to use this tense properly, it is useful to understand why this tense is being used. The box below illustrates the two completely different situations in which this tense is needed.

Present Perfect

The present perfect is formed with *have* or *has* and the past participle.

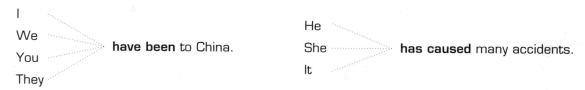

I
We
You
They
→ **have been** to China.

He
She
It
→ **has caused** many accidents.

When to Use the Present Perfect

There are two very distinct ways to use this tense:

1. Past Action Continues to the Present

Example: *Carmen **has lived** in Red Deer since 1991.*

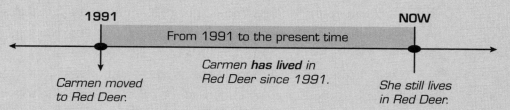

1991

From 1991 to the present time

NOW

Carmen moved
to Red Deer.

*Carmen **has lived** in
Red Deer since 1991.*

She still lives
in Red Deer.

Key words: never, ever, not ... yet, so far, up to now (from past to present time), since, for (period of time up to the present)

2. Past time(s) unknown

Example: *Charlie **has seen** the movie <u>Casablanca</u>. He **has seen** it three times.*

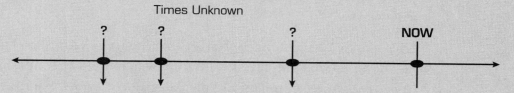

Times Unknown

?   ?   ?   **NOW**

*Charlie **has seen** the movie three times.*

Key words: already, once, twice, three times, many times... (before now)

You can also use the present perfect to describe recent events, with words like *recently, just, lately.*

EXERCISE 1

Subject and verb agreement review: circle the verb that should be used with the subject.

1. Both Rebeka and Diego *(is / are)* ready to leave now.

2. Who among us *(is / are)* best able to do the job?

3. There *(is / are)* many adult students in the college.

4. Everybody in the family *(is / are)* coming to the reunion.

5. Mathematics *(was / were)* one of his favorite subjects.

6. She's the type of person who *(lie / lies)* constantly.

7. Where *(is / are)* your hat and gloves?

8. Everyone in this room *(have / has)* to take responsibility for this mess.

9. Languages *(has / have)* been taught here for many years.

10. The furniture *(was / were)* stored in the basement locker.

11. Standing in front of the crowd *(was / were)* Stuart and his brother.

12. No one really *(expect / expects)* to win the prize.

13. The information that she gave me *(was / were)* very interesting and relevant.

14. A dictionary and a verb list *(is / are)* necessary in order to complete the test.

15. *(Has / Have)* anybody seen my car keys?

Present Perfect Tense: Question Form

Place the auxiliary *have* or *has* before the subject.

We (*have*) *known him for ten years.*   (*Have*) *we* **known** *him for ten years?*
                                                   How long **have** *we* **known** *him?*

Present Perfect Tense: Negative Form

Place *not* after the auxiliary *have*.

She has been to China.   *She has* **not** *been to China.*

Practice with the Present Perfect

Exercises 2 to 5 practice using the *present perfect where past action continues to the present.*

EXERCISE 2

Fill in the blanks using the present perfect tense only. Key words that indicate when the present perfect is used are in bold.

Dear Ginger,

How (you, be) _____ **lately**? I (miss) _____ you so much **since you went away**. (You, see) _____ any of your old friends **yet**? (You, go) _____ to any of your old haunts **yet**? Nothing (be) _____ the same here **since you left**. I (be, not) _____ able to get you out of my mind! I (walk) _____ all over town looking for faces that remind me of you, but I (find, not) _____ anybody, **yet**, who has red hair like yours. **In my life** I (never, see) _____ green eyes as lovely as yours. **So far**, you are the only woman that I (love, **ever**) _____ . Please come back soon. I know that you (be, not) _____ away **for long**, but I can't take it anymore. I need you.

Love Eddy

When to Use *For, Since,* and *Ago*

Since refers to a specific time in the past when the action began.

    Lois has worked at IBM **since** *1994.*

For refers to the amount of time that the action lasts. *For* can be used in other tenses.

Compare: *Clark worked at IBM* **for** *three years right after university.*

            Lois has worked at IBM **for** *three years.*

            Next summer, Suki will visit me **for** *three weeks.*

Ago refers to a time in the past when a completed action occurred.

    Clark left IBM 20 years **ago**.

EXERCISE 3

Fill in the blanks with *since, for,* or *ago.*

1. She has been asleep _____ hours.

2. Don't call him. He left two days _____ .

3. Clara has been acting that way _____ ages.

4. Mark hasn't washed his hair _____ last weekend.

5. Those children have had lice _____ several months.

6. I've lived in that house _____ I was a little kid.

7. A long time _____ an evil giant climbed down the beanstalk.

8. She's been ill ever _____ she had her tonsils out.

9. My uncle's had a cold _____ at least two weeks.

10. He hasn't called me _____ we graduated from high school.

EXERCISE 4

In the following exercise fill in the blanks with the simple past or present perfect tense.

1. Chandra and Jane (get) _____ engaged **three weeks ago**. They (be) _____ engaged **for three weeks**. They (be) _____ engaged **since the party**.

2. Aldo (come) _____ to Canada from Italy three months ago. Aldo (be) _____ in Canada for a few months.

3. Mr. and Mrs. Canuel (meet) _____ many years ago. They (know) _____ each other for over twenty years.

4. We (enter) _____ this class half an hour ago. We (be) _____ in this class for half an hour. We (be) _____ in our seats since 12:30.

EXERCISE 5

Proofread, and correct the error(s) in the following sentences. Highlight key words to help you decide the appropriate verb tense (key words are in bold in questions 1 and 2).

1. **Yesterday** I was waiting for my turn to use the banking machine when I've seen a robbery.

2. That is truly the best show that I've **ever** saw.

3. They have fought over money since many years.

4. Up to now, my parents have always treat me very well.

5. She is the sweetest child that I ever seen.

6. I'm sorry but I didn't finish my homework yet.

7. Walter has graduated from university last June.

8. Margaret is a secretary for twenty years.

9. I have seen Karen's new baby two weeks ago.

10. Since her remarriage Sally has try to become friends with her stepdaughter.

CLASS EXERCISE

Use either the present perfect or the simple past tense in the following sentences. Key words or phrases are in bold in number 1.

1. Judy (be) _____ in this town **for almost twenty years**. I (move) _____ here **one year ago**. I (meet) _____ Judy in an art class that I (take) _____ **last summer**. **When the course was over**, I (invite) _____ Judy for a coffee. We (be) _____ friends **ever since**.

2. My landlord, Mr. Selzer, knows Judy. He (know) _____ Judy for many years. He (teach) _____ Judy when she was in high school. She (be) _____ a very bad student, according to Mr. Selzer. Judy often (miss) _____ her math class when she was in high school.

3. Judy (see, not) _____ Mr. Selzer for many years. She never comes to my apartment building because she doesn't want to see her old math teacher. Last week, we (meet) _____ at the Cafe Santropol. After drinking some coffee, we (go) _____ to the Palace Theater.

4. At first, I (like, not) _____ this town but now that I (be) _____ here for one year, I (learn) _____ to love this place.

Present Perfect vs. Simple Past

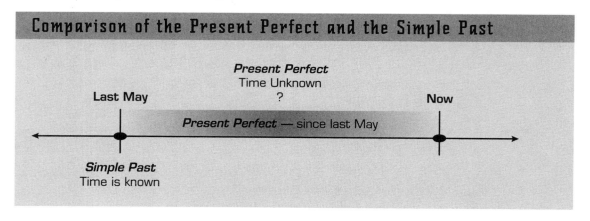

Present perfect tense is used:

1. when an action that began in the past continues to the present and possibly to the future.

*I **have been** in this seat for two hours.*

2. to talk about a completed past action (or actions) when we don't know or care about the time that the action occurred.

*Franz **has studied** over thirty types of poisonous plants.*

Simple past tense is used:

1. when an action is over and the time that the action occurred is known.

*Twenty years ago, Antonio **met** his wife Alicia.*

2. if the event happened at an understood time in the past.

***Did** you **put** away the bath towel?*

(Even if the time is not stated, if your mother asks you this question and both you and she are aware that you had a bath ten minutes earlier, then the past tense is used.)

3. if you are telling a story about an event that occurred completely in the past.

*Once upon a time, a small boy **lost** his way in the forest. Suddenly a...*

*When I was in Miami, I **saw** a shark the size of a small boat! The shark...*

Exercises 6 to 8 practice using the *present perfect where the past time is unknown.*

EXERCISE 6

Fill in the blanks with either the present perfect tense or the simple past tense.

1. Alfred (marry) _____ many women. He (marry) _____ Rosa in 1992.

2. Rosa (eat) _____ in every restaurant on Fifth Avenue. Rosa and I (eat) _____ at The Blue Lagoon Restaurant last New Year's Eve.

3. My brother (meet) _____ several famous people. My brother (meet) _____ Bob Dylan at a theater in 1984.

4. Lately my girlfriend and I (have) _____ trouble communicating. Just last week my girlfriend (throw) _____ a pillow at me.

5. Daniel and Julia (have) _____ at least twenty fights. Daniel is a big drinker. He (try) _____ to quit drinking several times. At the moment he doesn't drink. He (be) _____ on the wagon for about three weeks.

6. Mr. and Mrs. Arnold (be) _____ to New York twice. (you, think, ever) _____ about visiting New York?

7. I think that Robin (act) _____ in over fifteen movies. I (go) _____ to his latest movie last Thursday. I read that he (appear) _____ in several television shows.

EXERCISE 7

Fill in the blanks with either the present perfect tense, the simple past tense, or the past progressive tense.

1. Kevin (be) _____ a working artist for over ten years, but he (be, never) _____ able to support himself by selling his paintings. He (produce) _____ a lot of excellent work, and he (exhibit) _____ in several galleries in both Montreal and New York.

2. Kevin (receive) _____ a scholarship to study at an art college in Vancouver two years ago. As soon as he (get) _____ the money, he immediately (fly) _____ to Vancouver. After his arrival, while he (search) _____ for a cheap apartment, he (meet) _____ a girl called Holly. Holly (find) _____ a room for Kevin in the rooming house where she lives. Kevin (live) _____ in that rooming house ever since.

3. I (meet, never) _____ Holly. According to Kevin, Holly has skin the color of macaroni, hair the color of golden honey, and she is from a tiny town called Rattlesnake Hill. One day last year Kevin (notice) _____ a photograph on Terry's dresser. In the photo, Holly (stand) _____ next to a man. The man's muscled, tattooed arm (be) _____ around Holly.

4. Kevin (ask) _____ Holly who the man was. Holly (tell) _____ Kevin that the man is her brother, Frank. Apparently Frank is the mayor of Rattlesnake Hill. Frank (be) _____ the mayor of that town for several years. About four years ago, a doctor (remove) _____ Frank's tattoo with a laser.

EXERCISE 8

Write questions for the following answers using the appropriate tense. The answer to the question is in bold.

Example: Dorothy went to Oz **to see the Wizard**.

Why did Dorothy go to Oz?

1. Kathy has gained **15 pounds**.

_____

2. They slaughtered the pig **because they were hungry**.

_____

3. Rajiv has been to Malaysia **four times**.

_____

4. My brother owes me **two hundred dollars**.

_____

5. Jerry left the army in 1979. He stayed in the army **for three years**.

_____

6. Santiago is in the army. He has been in the army **for two years**.

_____

7. Karen quit smoking **eight years ago**.

_____

8. Ralph has smoked cigars **for thirty years**.

_____

CLASS EXERCISE

Proofread and correct the errors in the following sentences. If the sentence is correct, write *C* beside it. The first sentence has been corrected for you.

Example: Janice Joplin ⟨has⟩ died in 1971.
(Time is known so past tense must be used.)

1. Have you ever watch the show called *Mr. Bean*?

2. Since Kurt's death, his widow Courtney has a lot of trouble dealing with solitude.

3. When my mother was a child, she lived on a farm.

4. My brother Terry, who is the oldest child in my family, have been to NASA.

5. Last winter Tony has tried to get a better job.

6. So far this year, she has performed in two plays!

7. I must admit that I never seen a film as uplifting as *It's a Wonderful Life.*

8. I'm sorry, but you can't borrow that book. I haven't finished reading it yet.

9. I don't want to go to that movie with you because I already saw that film.

10. Once upon a time Snow White has met seven little dwarfs.

Present Perfect in the Passive Voice

You have seen that the passive voice is always formed with *be* and the past participle.

The present perfect is formed with *has* or *have* + *be* (*been*) + the past participle.

Active	Passive
Uri **has made** *many sales.*	*Many sales* **have been made** *(by Uri)*

EXERCISE 9

In the space below each sentence, identify the verb tense. Then change the active voice to the passive voice.

Example:

Active	**Passive**
The mice eat cheese every day.	*Cheese* **is eaten** *by the mice every day.*
Simple present tense	

1. Malaysian trees produce rubber.

_____

Rubber _____ by Malaysian trees.

2. Fred is using the computer.

_____

The computer _____ by Fred.

3. Inca Leathers made those belts.

_____

Those belts _____ by Inca Leathers.

4. At 10 p.m. John was fixing my car.

_____

At 10 p.m. my car _____ (by John).

5. Alberta has exported wheat for years.

_____

Wheat _____ by Alberta for years.

EXERCISE 10

Fill in the blanks with the correct tense in either the active or the passive voice.

1. In my father's home town, there are very few industries. The largest factory in town is the Winn Glass Factory. In fact, glass (produce) _____ by that company for over forty years. Every year, many of the local youth (hire) _____ by that factory when they finish high school.

2. My uncle (work) _____ at that company for over thirty years. Over the last few years production (cut) _____ to less than half of what it once was, so many local employees (lose) _____ their jobs. The union (go) _____ on strike several times since the factory opened.

CLASS EXERCISE

Continue filling in the blanks with the active or passive voice.

1. Sometimes accidents happen at the factory. Every day the glass (heat) _____ to such a high temperature that accidents can, and do, occur. My cousin (injure) _____ last March in a factory accident. On a regular basis all of the employees (tell) _____ by the bosses to sleep well and avoid alcohol before long shifts, but many of the employees (listen, not) _____ . Last March the bosses (ask) _____ by the employees' union to stay out the workers' private lives.

2. Since the recession, many "golden handshakes" (give) _____ to senior employees because the company is downsizing. Last June my aunt (ask) _____ my uncle to accept the golden handshake, but my uncle (want, not) _____ to retire at that time.

Present Perfect Progressive

The Present Perfect Progressive indicates that an action has been in progress from a past time up to the present.

It is formed with *have been* or *has been* + the *ing* form. The non-progressive verb list in Chapter 1 applies to this tense as it does to all progressive tenses. For example, you cannot say *I have been hating pizza for years* because *hate* is a non-progressive verb, and cannot be used in the *ing* form.

When to Use the Present Perfect Progressive

Use the present perfect progressive to emphasize the duration of an incomplete activity.

> I **have been driving** this car for eight hours.

The activity is still in progress, and the length of time spent doing the unpleasant chore is stressed.

You can also use the present perfect progressive to indicate that the results of an action are still visible.

> Somebody **has been sleeping** in my bed! The bed sheets are still rumpled.

> Somebody **has slept** in my bed. This could have happened yesterday.

With some verbs (*live*, *work*, *teach*) both the present perfect and the present perfect progressive have essentially the same meaning.

> I have lived here since 1994 = I **have been living** here since 1994.

EXERCISE 11

Now write questions with *How long*. Use the present perfect or the present perfect progressive.

Example: How Long

Right now Nanda is practicing his   *has he been practicing?*
trumpet playing.

1. His mother hates horn music.   _____

2. His mother is thinking of buying   _____
earplugs.

3. Nanda has a big problem.   _____

4. Nanda is tone deaf.   _____

5. His mother is looking for another   _____
instrument for her son.

6. Nanda wants a guitar.   _____

CLASS EXERCISE

Write the answer in the space provided.

1. Pierre has changed a tire.

Aziz has been changing a tire.

Whose clothes are more likely to be dirty?   _____

2. Mr. White has been drinking strong coffee.

   Mr. Green has drunk strong coffee.

   Who feels jittery now? _____

3. Marnie has yelled for twenty minutes.

   Natalia has been yelling for twenty minutes.

   Whose vocal cords are getting sore? _____

4. Mary has lived in Nova Scotia for years.

   Claire has been living in Nova Scotia for years.

   Is there any difference between these sentences? _____

EXERCISE 12

Use the present perfect or the present perfect progressive. In some cases, either tense may be used.

1. Mutt: Where is the subway?

   Jeff: The subway isn't far from here. I (walk) _____ there many times.

   Mutt: I'm getting tired. We (walk) _____ for six hours. You said that the subway wasn't far!

   Jeff: You're just out of shape. Well, here we are. Hey, Joe, how long (you, wait) _____ for the subway train?

   Joe: I (wait) _____ for about 10 minutes.

2. I'm going crazy. That baby (cry) _____ for two hours. I (see, never) _____ a baby that cries so much.

3. My hand is getting sore. I (write) _____ for two hours. I (write) _____ over one hundred invitations.

4. The Berezans (live) _____ on my street since 1976.

5. Jim: (be, you) _____ able to reach your sister on the phone yet?

   Bob: Not yet. I (try) _____ for the last 15 minutes.

4 The Past Perfect Tenses

The past perfect is formed with *had* and the past participle. For example: *Yesterday we went to see* Evita *even though we had seen it twice*.

As long as a story about a past event contains a very sequential order, you can probably stick to regular past tenses. However, sometimes you need to reach further back into the more distant past in order to explain something. For example:

> When we were children, Jack and I went for a walk in the fields near my farm. As we were passing a large rock, we heard a rattle. Beside the rock a rattlesnake was coiled up and ready to strike. Jack screamed with shock because he had never seen a snake before, but I remained calm, and we slowly backed up to get away from the snake. Afterwards, I teased Jack and mimicked his frightened reaction.

Jack's lack of experience with snakes predates the events in the story. Therefore, when you tell a story about a past event, you can use the past perfect to go back to an earlier past time.

When to Use the Past Perfect

The past perfect tense is used to place one past action before another. This tense is formed with *had* + past participle.

*Last night Robert couldn't pay for dinner because someone **had stolen** his wallet.*

Distant Past	**More Recent Past**	**NOW**
Before dinner someone had stolen his wallet	*Last night at dinner*	

CLASS EXERCISE

Do you understand the difference between the simple past and the past perfect? Answer the following questions and explain your answers.

1. When Sonia got to the 1996 Olympics in Atlanta, she had won a silver medal.

When Margaret got to the 1996 Olympics in Atlanta, she won a silver medal.

Who was already an Olympic champion when she got to the 1996 Olympics?

_____

_____

_____

2. When Andrew arrived at the theater, the music had started.

When Marcel arrived at the theater, the music started.

Who missed part of the show?

_____

_____

_____

3. At 8 o'clock this morning, Monica had her coffee.

At 8 o'clock this morning, Susan had had her coffee.

Who was drinking her coffee at 8 o'clock?

_____

_____

_____

4. When the second robbery occurred, Frank had just been arrested.

When the second robbery occurred, Phillip was arrested.

Who could not have committed the second robbery?

_____

_____

_____

5. Beth had the chicken pox when Pedro visited her.

Helen had had the chicken pox when Pedro visited her.

Who was sick in bed when Pedro visited?

_____

_____

_____

EXERCISE 1

Fill in the blanks with the simple past or the past perfect.

1. My sister (watch) _____ *Pulp Fiction* with me last night

even though she (see, already) _____ it twice.

2. When I (call) _____ Jennifer, her father (say)

_____ that she (move) _____

to Ottawa. I (just, want) _____ to know if Jennifer

had the novel *The Catcher in the Rye* that she (borrow)

_____ from me.

3. When we (arrive) _____ at the restaurant, our friends

(be) _____ no longer there. They (leave, already)

_____ . Later that night, we (call)

_____ them to apologize and also to find out why

they (wait, not) _____ for us.

4. Last Easter, my wife and I (cancel) _____ our flight to

Florida because the pilots (go) _____ on strike a week

earlier.

EXERCISE 2

Circle the correct verb tense to complete the sentences in the following paragraphs.

Yesterday my friend Tim (1. *quit / had quit*) his job. Many people thought that
Tim (2. *quit / had quit*) his job months ago. Tim loved his job, but to my knowledge
Tim (3. *made / had made*) several errors in the months before he left the job.

I'm sure that when Tim (4. *left / had left*) the office yesterday it (5. *was / had
been*) a very emotional moment for him. Last night I talked to Tim's wife about it.
When Tim (6. *arrived / had arrived*) home yesterday, he explained to his wife what he
(7. *did / had done*) and she (8. *told / had told*) him that she (9. *understood / had
understood*) completely.

CLASS EXERCISE

Fill in the blanks with the simple past or the past perfect tense.

1. Once upon a time there lived a man named Arthur, son of the king. Arthur (know, not) _____ that he was really the king's child because, in his entire life, he (live, never) _____ with the king. One day, quite by chance, Arthur (take) _____ part in a tournament to choose the next king. There was a contest: whoever could pull the magic sword, Excalibur, out of the stone would be declared the next king. Arthur (pull) _____ the sword out of the stone; therefore, Arthur (become) _____ king. Right after becoming king, Arthur (marry) _____ a beautiful woman named Guinevere, and later he (go) _____ off to war.

2. After the long war, Arthur (return) _____ home and (discover) _____ that his wife (become) _____ friends with a knight called Lancelot. Things started to go terribly wrong when Arthur (come) _____ upon Lancelot and Guinevere sleeping naked in the grass. Arthur left his sword next to them on the ground, to show the adulterous couple that he (see) _____ them, and then he left the scene. When Lancelot (awake) _____ from his lover's embrace, he realized, upon seeing the sword, that Arthur (be) _____ there. Lancelot immediately (run) _____ away.

Past Perfect Progressive

When to Use the Past Perfect Progressive

The past perfect progressive is used when one past action was in progress up to another specific past time. It is formed with *had been* + (verb)*ing*.

*Vincent **had been hiding** for weeks when, last Thursday, the police finally arrested him.*

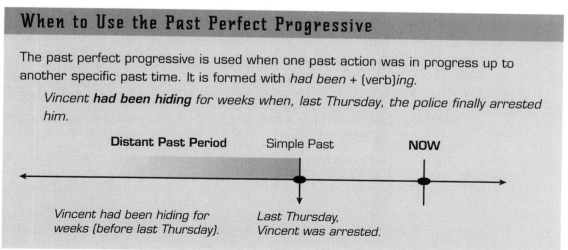

EXERCISE 3

Fill in the spaces with either the past perfect or the past perfect progressive.

1. Yesterday evening I was very tired because I (exercise) _____ for hours.

2. When the seven dwarfs returned home, they realized that someone (live) _____ in their home. They found a girl called Snow White in Grumpy's bed. She (sleep) _____ in his bed for several hours.

3. Last night my father put the cat out at 8 p.m. because the cat (be, not) _____ out all day. Not much later he opened the door and let the cat in because our crazy cat (meow) _____ for twenty minutes.

EXERCISE 4

Complete the exercise using any simple or progressive tense.

1. Last Friday, when I (arrive) _____ at the party, Alexia (wait) _____ for me. She (wait) _____ for two hours and she (be) _____ a little upset. When she saw me, she (run) _____ up to me and she told me that she (spend) _____ the evening all alone, because she (know, not) _____ anybody in the room.

2. I explained to her that I (lose) _____ the paper with the address of the party on it. I think that Alexia (wait) _____ at the party for a long time, because she was already a bit drunk.

Past Perfect Tenses in the Passive Voice

The passive form of the past perfect is formed with *had been* + the past participle.

Active: *Last night there was nothing left on the dinner table. My brother **had eaten** the food.*

Passive: *Last night there was nothing left on the dinner table. The food **had been eaten** by my brothers.*

5 The Future Tenses

The future tenses are relatively simple to use for intermediate-level students. When you use *will*, there are no verbs to conjugate, and no irregular verb lists to memorize. For example: *Next year I will move, my sister will stay here, my brother will buy a house, and we will remain close.* Notice that no *s* is necessary on third person singular verbs.

The future *be going to* form sometimes confuses students. Often students write *gonna* because that is what they hear English people saying. However, *gonna* is not a word and should not be written. Always use the form *is, am* or *are going to*.

Most of the time you can use both *will* and *be going to* to predict a future action, but, as is explained below, there are instances where either one or the other must be used.

Pay particular attention to the section entitled *Future Tenses: Time Clauses*, because there are cases where the future tense form cannot be used in English, even if it is used in other languages in the same situation.

Future

Will *vs.* Be Going To

Although both *will* and *be going to* can be used to make predictions about the future, there are some instances where you must use either one or the other.

Use *will* when you decide to do something at the time of speaking. You are "willing" to do it.

> The phone is ringing. I **will** answer it.

Use *be going to* when you have planned to do something before you talk about it.

> I**'m going to** visit Ottawa next week. I have my train ticket.

EXERCISE 1

Put the verb into the correct form, using *will* or *be going to*. In some cases, either one may be used.

1. I feel sick so I (visit) _____ the doctor.

2. The phone is ringing. I (get) _____ it.

3. Dorothy is pregnant. She (have) _____ a girl.

4. I have a lot of work to do so I (stay) _____ home tomorrow.

5. That's the doorbell. I (get) _____ it.

6. On my next vacation, I (visit) _____ Halifax. I have already bought the ticket.

7. I (make) _____ the coffee if you're too busy.

8. According to the radio broadcast, it (snow) _____ tonight.

9. Mike (do) _____ the dishes if you're too busy.

10. In the future I (be) _____ a lawyer or a notary.

Future Tenses: Time Clauses

In future sentences, use the present tense verb form after time markers.

I'll **call** you when I **get** home.

She **will meet** you as soon as she **finishes** work.

We **won't eat** supper until Anne **arrives**.

The rule applies for all verbs that follow these time markers:

when	before	as soon as	as long as
after	unless	until	in case
if			while

EXERCISE 2

Complete the following future tense sentences with the verbs in parentheses.

Example: Mary (come) *will come* if you (ask) *ask* her.

1. I (call) _____ you as soon as I (arrive) _____ in Paris next week.

2. When Monica (quit) _____ her job next Friday, everyone (be) _____ very happy.

3. I (eat) _____ the rest of the cake if you (finish) _____ the cookies.

4. Hugh (talk) _____ to Ron about it as soon as Ron (get) _____ here.

5. Anne (do) _____ the work alone unless she really (need) _____ us.

6. When I (have) _____ some spare time, I (help) _____ Toby with his math homework.

7. We (take care) _____ of the dog until the vet (arrive) _____ .

8. I (go, not) _____ unless you (go) _____ too.

9. As soon as the weather (get) _____ colder, Beth (go) _____ skiing with us.

10. We (prepare) _____ the meal tomorrow in case we (have, not) _____ time on the weekend.

Future Tenses in the Passive Voice

To form the passive voice in the future tense, simply write *will be* or *are going to be* + the past participle.

Active	Passive
Pierre **will do** the dishes later.	*The dishes **will be done** later (by Pierre).*
Alex is going to dry the dishes.	*The dishes **are going to be dried** (by Alex).*

EXERCISE 3

Change the following active sentences into the passive form. Use the appropriate verb tense.

Example: Jo is going to build our kitchen cabinets.

The kitchen cabinets are going to be built by Jo.

1. Someone will deliver the order.

_____

2. Jo's company, Woodwork, builds sturdy furniture.

_____

3. Last year Jo built a desk.

_____

4. The company will hire ten new people next year.

_____

5. Those new employees are going to need homes.

_____

Now change the following passive sentences to the active form.

Example: A new hockey arena is needed (by the town).

The town needs a new hockey arena.

6. Part-time jobs have been created by the government.

_____

7. Money is needed for the new hockey team.

_____

8. Money has been donated by the public.

_____

9. The project is going to be financed by the recreation committee.

_____

10. Parents will be invited to the opening of the new arena (by the organizers).

_____

CLASS EXERCISE

Part 1: Fill in the blanks with the present or future tense.

1. I've heard that banks are planning to replace all bank tellers with bank machines in the future. If the banks (replace) _____ tellers with machines, there (be) _____ disastrous consequences for the economy. When the tellers (have, not) _____ jobs anymore, they (need) _____ to receive government assistance, and every worker in Canada will have to pay for that.

2. Some banks claim that all tellers (retrain) _____ by the banks, and that very few people (lose) _____ their jobs, but I find that very hard to believe. When four or five people (run) _____ a bank branch instead of fifteen or twenty, then obviously many people (lay off) _____ by the banks!

Part 2: Proofread and correct any future tense errors.

3. The average consumer will also suffer if machines will replace humans. As soon as a person will need advice, or as soon as a customer will have a problem, it will take a machine longer to solve the problem.

4. A lot of people dislike dealing with a machine. The world will be a very impersonal place when all of our daily transactions will be done with a machine.

Embedded Questions

When a question is part of a larger sentence (embedded), no longer use the special question word order. An auxiliary after the question word is not needed.

Question	Embedded Question
Auxiliary	
What *do* you want for lunch?	He wonders *what you want for lunch.*

Use *if* or *whether* if there is no question word.

Auxiliary	
Did you finish your salad?	He wonders *if you finished your salad.*
Will you help me, please?	I want to know *whether you will help me.*

EXERCISE 4

Make a new sentence from these questions.

    Example: What does "itch" mean?

                I wonder *what "itch" means.*

1. What is Dan doing?

    She wants to know _____

2. Where does Dan live?

    She wonders _____

3. Why are the guests late?

    I would like to know _____

4. How long will the party last?

    He wonders _____

5. Does Gina smoke?

    Can you tell me _____

6. What is that police officer doing?

    She wonders _____

7. How long has he been there?

Do you know _____

8. What time did she leave?

Can you tell me _____

9. When will we leave?

I wonder _____

10. Is Kim going to watch the parade?

I would like to know _____

Present Tenses with a Future Meaning

You can use the present progressive tense to talk about a previously planned event.

> *This week, my son **is playing hockey** on Monday, and he **is going to** the dentist on Wednesday.*

You can use the simple present when you talk about schedules and timetables.

> *What time **does** the show **begin**?*
>
> *The train **leaves** at midnight.*
>
> *The football game **starts** at 2 p.m. tomorrow.*

EXERCISE 5

Complete the conversation with the words in parentheses. Use the present progressive or the simple present to indicate the future.

1. Kali: What (you, do) _____ this evening?

2. Sandra: Andrew and I (go) _____ to a play. Can you come with us?

3. Kali: I can't. I (take) _____ my little sister shopping.

4. Sandra: Well, the play (start) _____ at 7:30 p.m. Before the play we (plan) _____ to go to a coffee shop. Maybe we could all meet for coffee downtown.

5. Kali: How (you, go) _____ downtown? You (drive, not) _____ , are you? It's impossible to park downtown!

6. Sandra: No, we (drive, not) _____ . We (take) _____ the bus. It (leave) _____ every half hour.

Future Progressive vs. Future Perfect

These two future tenses can be tricky. Study the two boxes below, and see if you can make the distinction between the future progressive and the future perfect in the exercises that follow.

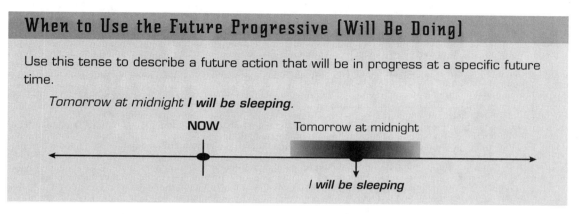

When to Use the Future Progressive [Will Be Doing]

Use this tense to describe a future action that will be in progress at a specific future time.

Tomorrow at midnight I will be sleeping.

NOW

Tomorrow at midnight

I will be sleeping

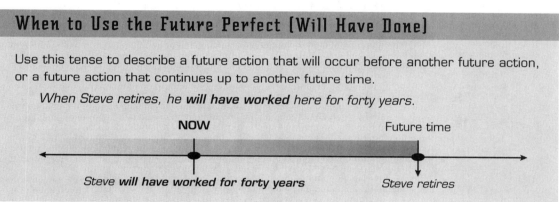

When to Use the Future Perfect [Will Have Done]

Use this tense to describe a future action that will occur before another future action, or a future action that continues up to another future time.

When Steve retires, he will have worked here for forty years.

NOW

Future time

Steve *will have worked for forty years*

Steve retires

CLASS EXERCISE

Answer the following questions.

1. Joe will be cooking supper when his wife arrives home from work.

Sam will have cooked supper when his wife arrives home from work.

Whose wife will eat first? _____

2. Next Saturday, Nadine will be finishing her work.

Next Saturday, Sandra will have finished her work.

Who gets to spend next Saturday relaxing? _____

3. Tonight at mealtime, Michael will have studied.

Tonight at mealtime, Diego will be studying.

Who will have his books at the supper table? _____

EXERCISE 6

Make sentences with the future perfect (will have done) or the future progressive (will be doing).

1. When I retire in the year 2020, I (work) _____ for 40 years.

2. On Sunday Gary plays chess from noon to 5 p.m., so on Sunday at 3:30 p.m. he (play) _____ chess.

3. Next month I (live) _____ with Gary for exactly 10 years.

4. I have only three dollars left in my bank account. If I'm not careful, I (spend) _____ all my money before my next paycheck comes!

5. Don't plan to watch the news at my place tonight. By 10 p.m. I (go) _____ to bed.

6. When I retire, in 25 years, I (work) _____ for more than half my life.

7. I have to work late this evening, so if you try to call me at 7 p.m., I (work) _____ .

8. By the time we finish the project, it (take) _____ over three years to complete.

9. What (you, do) _____ tomorrow at noon?

10. Tomorrow when I arrive at the station, my mother's train (arrive) _____ and she (wait) _____ for me in the station's restaurant. By the time we get home from the station, Mom (tell) _____ me all of the family gossip.

CLASS EXERCISE

Find and correct the errors, if necessary.

1. She will help us finish the job unless she will be too tired.

2. By tomorrow, Angie has been in Canada for exactly four years.

3. I will apply for a job when I will finish my schooling.

4. I go to bed at 10 p.m. Tonight at midnight I will sleep.

5. When I will get home later, I will phone my mother.

6. By the year 2010, she will be a scientist for 30 years.

7. In case you will not have any spare time, I will mow the lawn.

8. The phone is ringing. I am going to answer it!

9. I will listen to the radio while you are going to fix the television.

10. We won't eat dinner until Allison will arrive.

Review of Sections 1 to 5

CLASS EXERCISE A: PRESENT TENSES REVIEW

Fill in the blanks with the simple present or the present progressive tense. (20 points)

1. Judy: What (happen) _____ with you these days?

2. Maya: Not much. Look over there! What (that girl, try) _____ to do?

3. Judy: I (think) _____ that she is in trouble. What (she, say) _____ to that man over there?

4. Maya: I (know, not) _____ . Maybe she (tell) _____ him to get lost.

5. Judy: Oh look. The man (leave) _____ . He (seem) _____ to be in a hurry. (you, suppose) _____ he is dangerous?

6. Maya: Well, he (appear) _____ to be a little eccentric. He (wear) _____ orange cowboy boots, and he (have) _____ a feather in his cap. Now the girl (walk) _____ towards us. (you, know) _____ her?

7. Judy: No. Maybe she (know) _____ that we (discuss) _____ her. What (you, think) _____ she (want) _____ with us?

8. Maya: Maybe she simply (want) _____ to know why we (stare) _____ at her.

CLASS EXERCISE B: SUBJECT-VERB AGREEMENT

Add *s* to all third-person singular verbs. The verb *be* has already been conjugated. There are 14 verbs to conjugate.

(1) A study have been made by a primatologist who look at the way that gorillas interact. The study focus on a group of gorillas from a central African nation. A group from the U.S.A. regularly send money for the study and supply the female primatologist, Ms. Windlow, with equipment and staff. Her equipment include tents, a computer, a fax machine and cooking equipment. Ms. Windlow hire local people to help find and examine the gorillas. The research grant contain extra money so that the primatologist can go home twice a year.

(2) The research focus on one particular group of gorillas. The study examine the social hierarchy in that gorilla group, and explain how one young female gorilla take care of her babies. Although there is sporadic fighting in the region, the primatologist insist that she is completely safe, and she absolutely refuse to leave the area.

CLASS EXERCISE C: PAST TENSES REVIEW

Underline and correct the past tense errors in the following sentences.

1. Jamie didn't wanted to go to the show yesterday.

2. The two best things about my previous job was that I could get free hockey tickets, and that I had Fridays off.

3. While Bill frying something on the stove, the fire alarm went off. We call the alarm our "burnt-food detector."

4. Why didn't he stay at the farm with us last night? Didn't you asked him to join us?

5. Yesterday, we were receiving a very disturbing letter from our bank.

6. The young couple didn't noticed that their car was being towed away.

7. At last night's party, when the police arrived, 40 people danced in the room.

8. Although I rarely read novels, last week I choosed to read Winston Groom's novel, *Forrest Gump*.

9. Where you found the Winston Groom novel? Was it in the library?

10. There was several copies of the novel in the main branch of the library.

CLASS EXERCISE D: PRESENT, PAST, AND PRESENT PERFECT REVIEW

Write the verbs in the correct tense in the space provided.

Dear Shyamal,

Thank you for your letter. I realize that I (write, not) _____ to you for many years. I (have, not) _____ an excuse for that, other than to say that in recent years my life (become) _____ increasingly busy. I (have) _____ a full-time job and two children, but I know that I really have no excuse for not writing.

I imagine that your life (change) _____ a lot since our last meeting. How (everybody, do) _____ over there? I (be, not) _____ back to Asia since that first voyage twelve years ago.

India (undergo) _____ many changes since my visit there. When I (visit) _____ you in 1984, almost nobody had televisions. At that time, the Indian government (allow, not) _____ foreign-made electrical goods into India. During my year in India, I once (meet) _____ an American girl on a bus who, at that moment, (smuggle) _____ a Japanese-made VCR into India. The laws (change) _____ in recent years, and now foreign goods can be imported into India.

(you, be) _____ to Shantiniketan recently? That was one of the most beautiful places that I (ever, see) _____ . In fact, I (be, never) _____ to a village or town since then that could compare.

CLASS EXERCISE E: QUESTIONS PRACTICE

Write the questions for the following answers. The specific answer is in bold.

1. Willy has been a carpenter **for twelve years**.

_____

2. Nadine bought **some used books** when she was in Boston.

_____

3. Elsa asked **Richard** to go to the party with her.

_____

4. The baby has been sleeping **for four hours**.

_____

5. Vincent does the dishes **every morning at 6 a.m.**

_____

6. Trish and Elise have been to **20 countries**.

_____

7. Last winter, we stayed in Mexico City **for two months**.

_____

8. **Alicia** gave me that leather handbag yesterday.

_____

9. The museum is about **four kilometers** from Alicia's home.

_____

10. Karen goes to her doctor **every six months**.

_____

CLASS EXERCISE F: ALL TENSE REVIEW

Highlight the tense that is most appropriate. (20 answers)

1. Right now Fred (_is preparing / prepare / prepares_) dinner. Tim isn't helping because he (_has / have / is having_) a cold.

2. The phone is ringing again. I (_am going to answer / will answer_) it, unless you (_think / will think_) it is for you.

3. In 1992, when Dominique started working at the advertising agency, she (_never used / has never used / had never used_) a computer before. Now she is very good on the computer because she (_use / is using / uses_) one every day.

4. While William (_washing / was washing / washed_) the dishes last night, I (_hear / heard / was hearing_) a loud crash. I (_run / ran / have run / had run_) into the kitchen and almost cried because he (_had dropped / has dropped / dropped_) our brand new crystal bowl.

5. When I bumped into my childhood friend on the street last week, we (_don't recognized / didn't recognize / hadn't recognized_) each other immediately. When he began to talk to me, I realized that I (_saw / have seen / had seen_) him before because I (_recognized / have recognized / had recognized_) his voice. Next Tuesday, we (_meet / are going to meet / will meet_) for coffee at Murray's Café, unless something unexpected (_will come / is going to come / come / comes_) up.

6. Marco always (_act / acts / is acting_) very inconsistently. Some days, when I (_passed / pass / passes_) him in the hall, he (_smile / smiles / is smiling_), and says "hello." But on other days, he is downright rude. Tomorrow, when I (_will see / see / sees_) him, he probably (_doesn't greet / won't greets / won't greet_) me.

CLASS EXERCISE G: ALL TENSES REVIEW (INCLUDING PASSIVE VOICE)

Fill in the blanks with the appropriate tense. The verb may be in the active or the passive voice. (15 answers)

1. When she was a teenager Carolyn and her boyfriend (involve)

_____ in several crimes. Although Carolyn (never, arrest)

_____ during her teen years, her boyfriend Carl (arrest)

_____ several times since 1985. Now Carol has her act

together, and last year she (hire) _____ at a graphic

design company. She (see, not) _____ Carl since 1992,

even though he (try) _____ on several occasions to

contact her.

2. Traditionally, soldiers who (conscript) _____ are

youthful. My great uncle was only eighteen when he (go)

_____ to fight in World War II. When he was sent

overseas, (never, see) _____ death, and he (traumatize)

_____ by what he saw in Europe. He is now a very old

man, and he rarely (discuss) _____ the war years.

3. More individuals in our society will lose hope if we (neglect)

_____ to address the unemployment issue. A great

number of companies (downsize) _____ since the

1980's, and this is contributing to the high unemployment rate.

4. Since the 1970's, disaster films (be) _____ very popular.

Almost every natural catastrophe (explore) _____ by

American filmmakers, including floods, tornadoes, and fires.

Tense Review Chart

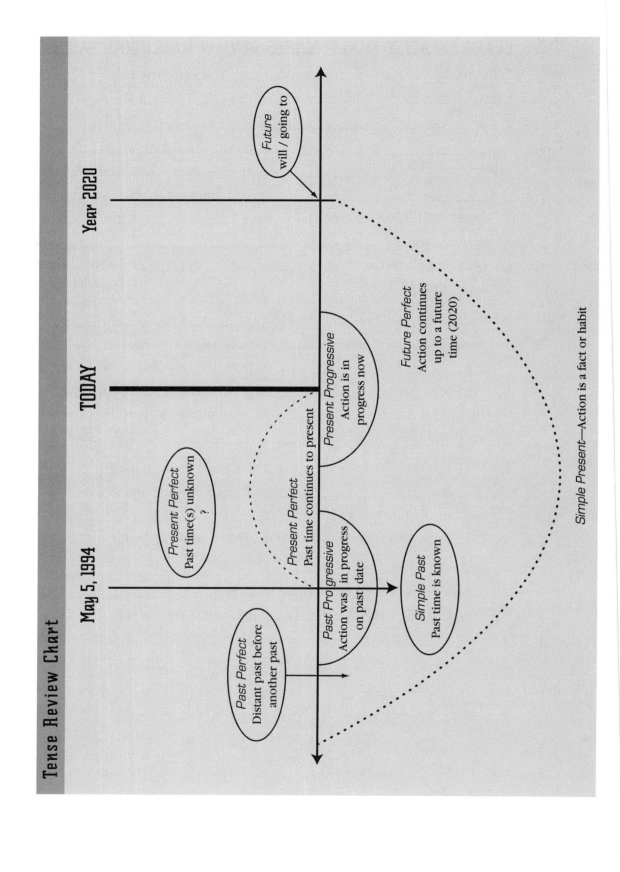

CLASS EXERCISE H: ALL TENSES REVIEW

Using the verb chart to help you, name the tense used in each of the following sentences. Then, in the space provided, briefly state *why* that tense was used.

	Verb Tense	Why Tense was Used
	Simple present	*Action is a fact*

1. Humans **need** food and water to survive.

2. My day usually **begins** with a cup of coffee and toast.

3. I **am presently working** as a fashion designer.

4. I **started** my job on May 5, 1994.

5. On that day in 1994, I **was walking** past this building when I saw a sign in the window.

6. I **had never worked** as a designer before then.

7. I **have been** at this company since 1994.

8. My boss and I **have gone** to Paris several times on business trips.

9. I **will probably quit** my job in the year 2020.

10. By the time that I quit, I **will have worked** for most of my life in the fashion industry.

6 Problems with Plurals

Students may feel comfortable with their use of regular and irregular plural nouns. However, there are some problems that even advanced students sometimes have with plurals. For example, in both Spanish and French, adjectives take a plural form. But *las cosas bonitas* and *les belles choses* become *beautiful things* in English, because English adjectives don't have plural forms.

This section contains four rules, given in the "Plural Tip" boxes.

Irregular Plurals

Plural Tip 1

Irregular plurals do not need an additional *s*.

EXERCISE 1

Write the plural form of the following nouns in the spaces provided.

1. man _____

2. goose _____

3. child _____

4. woman _____

5. gentleman _____

6. person _____

One Of The ... *and* Each/Every

> ## Plural Tip 2
>
> Always follow *one of the ...* with a plural noun.
>
> > **One of the best <u>movies</u>** *that I've ever seen is called Dr. No.*
> >
> > **One of my favorite <u>actors</u>** *is Sean Connery.*
> >
> > *India is* **one of the most interesting <u>countries</u>** *in the world.*
>
> *Each* and *every* are always followed by a singular noun.
>
> > *I love you with* **each <u>fiber</u>** *of my body.*
> >
> > *Donald has been to* **every Woody Allen <u>film</u>**.

EXERCISE 2

Each sentence has one plural error. Circle the error, and write the correct word in the space provided.

1. You must study each grammar rules very carefully. _____

2. Those parents think that their children's want too many Christmas presents. _____

3. Although it is disturbing for us, many directors like to make violent film. _____

4. Every Christmas the childrens make their parents take them to see Santa Claus. _____

5. One of the best director in the world will be at the Montreal Film Festival. _____

6. There is a big difference between men who like women and the one who don't. _____

7. I will show you some example of how people write incorrectly. _____

8. There are a lot of show on TV that are very bad. _____

9. One of the most interesting special that I've ever seen was on PBS TV. _____

10. Criminals often have many reason for their evil actions. _____

11. The people who live in those small houses take good care of each others. _____

12. Every characters in that TV show is really funny. _____

Non-count Nouns

Plural Tip 3

Non-count nouns do not take a plural form.

If you can't put a number directly before a noun (a person, place or thing), then it cannot be counted.

Look at the differences in these sentences:

1. Those tables are very expensive. I'm going to buy two tables.
2. That furniture is very expensive. I'm going to buy some furniture.

In the first sentence, *tables* can be counted. It takes an *s*. In the second sentence, *furniture* cannot be counted, so it cannot take an *s*. If you want to count a non-count noun, you must begin with an expression like "one piece of," "twenty pieces of."

Some Non-count Nouns

Non-count nouns include "category" names (such as *mail*) which cannot be counted. *Types* of mail can be counted, however (letter, package, etc. .)

luggage	news	equipment
jewelry	furniture	music
homework	machinery	money

Non-count nouns also include abstract nouns, such as the following:

advice	education	evidence
information	health	help
knowledge	violence	research

With non-count nouns, use *much* and *a little*.

> How **much homework** do you have?   I just have a **little homework** tonight.

With count nouns use *many* and *a few*.

> How **many suitcases** do you have?   I just have a **few bags**.

EXERCISE 3

Write *much* or *many* in the spaces provided.

1. How _____ money do you have in your wallet?

2. How _____ electricity do you need to power that stove?

3. Carl is a loner. He doesn't have _____ friends.

4. The dog is shedding its hair. It doesn't have _____ hair left.

5. There isn't _____ information that I can give you. Call back later.

6. How _____ luggage do you have? Do you have _____ suitcases?

7. There are _____ houses in that new development. Unfortunately, there are too _____ acts of violence in that town.

8. I thought you said that there isn't _____ violence around this area?

9. How _____ pages of homework do you have tonight?

10. My late grandfather didn't have _____ different jobs in his life. Because there wasn't _____ work available, he remained a farmer throughout his life.

Write *a few* or *a little* in the spaces provided.

11. We need _____ more hangers in this closet.

12. Could you give me _____ help? I can't start my car.

13. Pilo knows _____ French grammar. He knows _____ words in English.

14. Can you lend me _____ more money? I need _____ more dollars.

15. I can meet you for _____ minutes. I have _____ free time now.

Adjectives

> ### Plural Tip 4
>
> Adjectives (which describe nouns) do not take a plural form.
>
>   Incorrect: *Those are the problems students.*
>   Correct: *Those are the **problem** students.*

Be aware that adjectives may appear after the verb *be*.

Those cars are **expensive**.

Your ideas are **very interesting**.

CLASS EXERCISE

Try using these adjectives in a short descriptive paragraph. You could describe a close friend or family member.

Some Adjectives					
Personality Traits		**Physical Appearance**		**Physical Traits**	
sensitive	selfish	striking	tall	whiskery	
sensible	proud	handsome	slender	wrinkled	
gentle	nervous	homely	plump	dimpled	
kind	flighty	overweight	heavy set	balding	
rude	obnoxious	skinny	muscular	curly (hair)	
stingy	witty	pale	athletic		
sympathetic	easygoing	gorgeous		hazel (eyes)	
friendly	shy			cleft (chin)	

EXERCISE 4

There are errors in these sentences of the following types: incorrect plural form or the incorrect use of *much* or *many*. If the sentence is correct, write *C* in the space provided. If the sentence has an error, correct it in the space provided.

1. There are many unexplained naturals events.   *natural events* _____

2. It's possible that one day there will be no more whale.   _____

3. Santa brings hope to every childrens in the world.   _____

4. Teenagers are causing too much accidents.   _____

5. It's important for many children to be at the party.   _____

6. In *Dumb and Dumber*, Harry and Lloyd dream of being earth worms breeders.   _____

7. There are a lot of TV shows that are really stupids.   _____

8. I carefully watched each moments of the play.   _____

9. Salinger is one of the best writer of this century.   _____

10. We search for some simples explanations about the meaning of life.   _____

11. Her questions are always very intelligents.   _____

12. She doesn't have much informations to give you. _____

13. Gerry has many funny pieces of advice to give you. _____

14. There isn't many violence in these streets. _____

15. That is one of the worst show on television. _____

CLASS EXERCISE: PLURAL FORM

Add *s* to any noun that requires a plural form, or rewrite the noun in its irregular plural form. There are 15 nouns that must be changed from the singular to the plural form.

"Many *child* have no food" would be changed to "Many *children* have no food."

(1) At the present time, there are very few job available. Many person have decided to create their own job. Here are some simple piece of advice that could help you to plan your own business.

(2) First, you have to think of something that isn't already being done extensively. If you want to break into an existing market, it's a good idea to create new contact, and to verify if one of your competitor is already in the region.

(3) If possible, try to develop a product that doesn't already exist. Original idea, like the one by the creator of the hula hoop, can seem simple, yet this idea eventually turned the inventor into a millionaire. Although you can't expect to earn two million dollar immediately, you can expect to turn a profit in the long term. An accountant once told me that every new business should have a four-year plan. In other word, it could take four year before the business hits the break-even point.

(4) Many people always forget an important step. They forget to ask knowledgeable individual for information and piece of advice. We can't all be good in every field, and we must recognize our weakness and be prepared to ask for help.

(5) If you lack information in a particular area, you could take extra course in your free time. You don't have to hurry. You may need to take several year to plan your business. It can take a lot of time to complete a project successfully.

Modals

Modals (or modal auxiliary verbs, as they are also known) are used when we say that events are possible or probable, or when we want to refer to willingness, ability, obligation or advice.

Don't add *s* to modals or to the verbs that follow them, because modals have no *s* form for the third person singular. For example: *I should work late and Sharon must stay here. The boss could let us leave but he wouldn't do that.* Notice that none of the auxiliaries or verbs have an *s*.

The idiom *have to* has been added to the following list of modals, mainly because it has the same meaning as another modal, and means *necessity*. However, *have to* is not, strictly speaking, a modal, and it does have a third person singular form, *has to*, which is used with *he*, *she* and *it*. Unlike other modals, *have to* requires the auxiliary *do* or *does* in the question and negative forms.

Just as modals don't change to take an *s*, the actual modal also doesn't change when you talk about a past time. You either use another modal (for example, *I can speak German* becomes *I could speak German* in the past time) or you add *have* and the past participle to the modal to indicate a past time (for example, *She should sleep* becomes *She should have slept* in the past time).

The modal *shall* has not been included on the list mainly because it is rarely used in North America. However, if you are interested, *shall* could be used in place of *should* when asking a polite question. *Shall I help you? Shall* can also be used instead of *will* to indicate a future action (for example, *I shall phone you tomorrow*).

Using Modals

Modals in Present and Past Tenses

Summary of Modals in Present and Past Tenses			
Modal Form	**Usage**	**Present Tense**	**Past Tense**
Can	*ability*	She **can** speak German.	could speak
Could	a) *possibility* b) *polite request*	Alice **could** lend you $10. **Could** I borrow a $20?	could have lent
Should	a) *giving advice* b) *expectation*	You **should** see a doctor. The storm **should** hit soon.	should have seen
Ought to	*same meaning as "should"*	You **ought** to see a doctor.	ought to have seen
May	a) *possibility* b) *polite request*	It **may** be a mouse. **May** I help you?	may have been
Might	*possibility*	I **might** go to a movie.	might have gone
Must	a) *necessity* b) *probability*	You **must** do your work. She **must** be ill.	had to do must have been
Would	a) *conditional* b) *preference* c) *polite request*	She **would** call if . . . I **would rather** have a tea. **Would** you like a cup of tea?	would have called
Have to	*necessity*	She **has to** work late.	had to work

ORAL ACTIVITY

Answer the following questions.

1. Which two have the same meaning?
   a. John ought to pay for the sitter.
   b. John could pay for the sitter.
   c. John should pay for the sitter.

2. Which sentence is most polite? Least polite?
   a. May I use your phone?
   b. Can I borrow your phone?
   c. Could I borrow your phone?

3. Which two have the same meaning?
   a. That bank might close this year.
   b. That bank must close this year.
   c. That bank may close this year.

4. Which employee had no choice?
   a. Jose had to run home.
   b. Martin must have run home.
   c. Anne had better run home.

5. Which speaker is most certain?
   a. Nadia: That black spot must be ink.
   b. Rosy: That black spot has to be ink.
   c. Aline: That black spot may be ink.

6. Which person has a choice?
   a. The doctor must work overtime.
   b. The nurse may stay late tonight.
   c. The orderly has to work all night.

Modals: Question Form

All modals (except *have to*) act as auxiliaries. To form a question, move the modal before the subject.

Statement	Question form
I (can) hear you.	(Can) you hear me?
She **should** eat those carrots.	**Should** she eat those carrots?
Henry has to work late.	**Does** Henry **have to** work late?

EXERCISE 1

Make questions for the following answers. The specific answer to the question is in bold.

1. **Yes**, Diego should go to the hospital.

_____

2. He has to go there **tomorrow**.

_____

3. **No**, he can't eat or drink after midnight.

_____

4. Well, he should bring **slippers** with him.

_____

5. **Yes**, he has to go into the operating room without his parents.

_____

6. His parents must wait **outside** the operating room during the operation.

_____

7. **Yes**, they can go into the recovery room with him.

_____

Modals: Negative Forms

Examine the negative forms of the following modals. Notice that *have to* needs an auxiliary.

Statement	Negative	Negative contraction
He should work harder.	He **should not** work harder.	*shouldn't*
He could have stayed home.	He **could not have stayed** home.	*couldn't have stayed*
Brian has to do it.	Brian **does** not **have to** do it.	*doesn't have to*

EXERCISE 2

Make the modals in the following sentences negative.

Example: Eric should call me.   *should not call (or shouldn't)*

1. Melanie has to exercise more often.   _____

2. Ellen can help him.   _____

3. Rebecca would like a coffee.   _____

4. Helen had to phone home right away.   _____

5. The cat could be at the neighbor's house.   _____

6. Isaac should have done his homework yesterday.   _____

7. She could have done more work.   _____

8. He must have seen the accident.   _____

CLASS EXERCISE

Does *must* indicate (*P*) Probability or (*N*) Necessity in the following sentences?

Example: Someone is at the door. It must be Simon.   _____*P*_____

1. Carol isn't home. She must still be at school.   _____

2. He must run to the toilet because he feels ill.   _____

3. That light must be a UFO. There is no other explanation. _____

4. Those lizards must live in a warm environment or they will die. _____

5. The spots on your sleeve must have been ketchup from your hot dog. _____

EXERCISE 3

Change the sentences to the past tense. Remember to use the appropriate past form of *must*.

Must meaning *Necessity*: past form is *had to*
Must meaning *Probability*: past form is *must have* + past participle

Example: Monica *has to help* the patients.   *had to help* _____

1. Her brother *must be* in an accident.   _____

2. Her brother, Terry, *has to get* stitches.   _____

3. Kevin *should clean* his hair thoroughly.   _____

4. Kevin *must have* lice.   _____

5. Pepino *could help* us.   _____

6. Arnold *must work* overtime. (He has no choice.) _____

7. The doctors *should be* more careful.   _____

8. Dr. Levine *doesn't have to work* today. _____

9. Alex *can't find* the maternity ward. _____

10. Frank *shouldn't worry* so much. _____

11. Clara *should try* to get more exercise. _____

12. The noise in the wall *may be* a mouse. _____

12. What else *could* the noise *be?* _____

14. Barnie *can answer* the phones. _____

15. *Could* John *help* us to push the car? _____

EXERCISE 4

Circle and correct the errors in the following sentences.

1. Francine should has known better than to drink and drive. She is 40 years old!

2. I don't understand why a hockey player would earned such a big salary!

3. On the Internet you can send and received e-mail.

4. Your screenplay is good, but the movie should ended in a tragedy.

5. They held a tournament to discover who can slay the dragon.

6. When their sick mother fell asleep yesterday, the children should not made so much noise.

EXERCISE 5

Fill in the blanks using modals. Sometimes there may be more than one choice.

1. Paula has salty fingers that smell like vinegar. She (eat) _____ the salt and vinegar chips!

2. You (tell, not) _____ Celine about the party! It was supposed to be a surprise!

3. When I was younger, I (do) _____ one hundred sit-ups. Now I (do, not) _____ twenty of them.

4. Excuse me. (make, I) _____ an appointment to speak to Mr. Bindi, please?

5. I was caught driving without a seatbelt last month, and I (pay) _____ a big fine, so I went to City Hall yesterday to pay it.

6. I'm sorry, but I (leave) _____ now. I have no choice.

A conversation between a customer (C) and a store clerk (SC)

7. C: Excuse me, but (you, help) _____ me? I (find, not) _____ any writing paper.

8. SC: You (look) _____ in aisle 2, next to the pens and pencils.

9. C: I have looked there already. There isn't any unlined writing paper. I (buy) _____ *unlined* writing paper.

10. SC: Why (it, be) _____ be unlined?

11. C: Well, my teacher asked us to buy unlined paper. She told us that we (find) _____ it here.

12. SC: Well, your teacher (make) _____ a mistake! We never have unlined writing paper. You (try) _____ the store across the street.

Modals in the Passive Voice

Summary of Modals in the Passive Voice

Active	Passive
	modal + *be* + the past participle
Harold **should do** the job alone.	*The job **should be done** alone.*
People **must take off** their boots.	*Boots **must be taken off** at the door.*
Someone **can use** the phone now.	*The phone **can be used** now.*
The judge **ought to send** him to prison.	*He **ought to be sent** to prison.*
He **has to pay** the dentist.	*The dentist **has to be paid**.*

Note: For most past form modals, use modal + *have been* + past participle.
Jake must have eaten the pizza.   *The pizza must have been eaten.*

EXERCISE 6

Complete the passage using the active or passive form of the modal and verb. Be sure that you have used the correct tense.

1. Virtual reality is a new technology that lets you experience, in three dimensions, a simulated reality. Virtual reality (can, use) _____ by everybody. In my opinion the technology (should, use) _____ only for altruistic reasons. For example, in medicine the technology (could, enable) _____ surgeons to visualize complicated surgical procedures.

2. Unfortunately, this technology has already been used for morally questionable purposes. There is speculation that, in the past, some armies, (may, train) _____ their soldiers by using that technology.

3. Presently, this technology (can, incorporate) _____ into the training of soldiers in the several ways. The soldier (may, believe) _____ that he or she is shooting at a "virtual body," yet the body would look almost exactly like a real person. This (could, use) _____ as a method of desensitizing young soldiers.

CLASS EXERCISE

Fill in the blanks with the active or the passive form of the modal and verb. Be sure that you have used the correct tense.

Kara, my four-year-old sister (1. can, go, not) _____ outside yesterday. She (2. have to, stay) _____ in bed because she had a flu bug. She (3. can, not, get) _____ out of bed because she felt so weak. She also had a high fever. Her temperature (4. have to, take) _____ every four hours by my mother. Kara (5. can, not, give) _____ any solid foods. She (6. should, have) _____ some medicine to reduce her fever but she didn't want any. Last night, at about 10 p.m., she (7. have to, bring) _____ to the hospital by my father, because her fever was so high. She was so weak at that time that she (8. have to, carry) _____ into the hospital by my father.

Conditional Sentences

Conditional sentences have two parts. The main clause depends on the condition set in the *if* clause.

Main clause	*If* clause
Mary will help us	if we ask her.
Pedro would visit you	if you invited him.
Carolyn would have called	if she had had more time.

The problems with conditional sentences occur when we change the type of condition. If something is possible, the conditional form is easy to create. The type of sentence becomes more complicated when we talk about something that is not really probable, or about something in the past that is impossible.

Possible Future

In Possible Future sentences, the condition is something that will probably happen.

*If you **brush** your teeth after every meal, you **will get** fewer cavities.*

If & present tense ⟶ future tense

EXERCISE 1

Complete the sentences below. The following sentences express possible situations.

1. I have been working overtime lately. If my boss (give) _____ me a few days off, I will call you at your country house. If you need any groceries brought to the country house, just call me, and I (bring) _____ them to you.

2. If the weather (be) _____ nice next weekend, we will have a soccer practice. If it (rain) _____ , the practice (be) _____ canceled.

3. You (learn, not) _____ how to play the piano if you (practice, not) _____ . If you (try) _____ to play the scales every day, you (improve) _____ a lot.

Unlikely Present

In Unlikely Present sentences, the condition is something that is very improbable.

> If I **won** a million dollars in the lottery, I **would buy** a new car.
>
> If I **won** a lot of money, I **could buy** a new house.

The odds of winning the lottery are very remote. In these types of sentences, we simply express a wish about an unlikely situation.
Would expresses the intention to do something.
Could expresses the possibility of doing something.

In the *if* clause, the past verb tense is used. With the verb *be*, use the *were* form with all subjects. (In colloquial or "street" English, you occasionally hear *was*.)

> If I **were** you, I **would stop** smoking.
>
> If she **were** a bit older, she **would behave** much better.

> If & past tense ——→ would (stop / quit / find …)
> were

EXERCISE 2

Complete the sentences below. Each sentence expresses an unlikely situation.

1. If I won a million dollars in the lottery, I (build) _____ myself a large house, and I (put) _____ a large art room on the top floor. The art room (have) _____ large windows on every wall.

2. Kira works long days at the factory, and she barely makes ends meet. Kira would visit us more often if she (have) _____ just a little more free time. Kira's boss is very unreasonable. If I (be) _____ Kira, I (look) _____ for another job.

3. Selvan says that he (fly) _____ to Sri Lanka if he had the money. Unfortunately, he doesn't have enough money right now. If I (be) _____ rich, I (give) _____ him a plane ticket so that he could visit his family.

CLASS EXERCISE

In each of the following sentences, decide whether the situation is possible or unlikely, and choose the correct form of the verb.

> Possible Future: *If* & present tense ⟶ future tense
> Unlikely Present: *If* & past tense ⟶ would (stop / quit / find ...)
> were

1. Errol really loves you. He will marry you if you just (ask) _____ him. I know he will. If I (be) _____ you, I would propose to him.

2. The band (play) _____ at the Spectrum for another night if they have time in their schedule. If it were possible, the crowd (ask) _____ that band to perform for 20 shows.

3. If Mrs. Lacombe were my mother, I (ask) _____ her for a really big allowance. I know that I can't ask my mother for more money. If my mother (have) _____ the money, I know that she would give it to me, but my mother (have, not) _____ extra money.

4. I'm looking for a job so that I can help my mother with expenses. If I (can) _____ work anywhere, I would work as a highly paid musician, but that's just a dream. In the real world, I think that Mr. Burger will hire me. If he (give) _____ me a job at his restaurant, I will buy groceries for my family, and if I (have) _____ extra money after that, I (pay) _____ for my university tuition.

Impossible Past

In Impossible Past sentences, the condition is something that cannot happen, because the event is over. The speaker expresses regret about a past event, or expresses the wish that a past event had worked out differently.

> If I **had known** that he was dying, I **would have forgiven** him!

> If you **had completed** your assignments, you **would have passed** the course.

> If & past perfect tense ⟶ would have (past participle)

CLASS EXERCISE

The following situations occurred, and cannot be changed. However, we can dream about changing the past. For each situation, write an impossible past conditional statement.

For example:

Mr. Tanguay won last fall's election because he promised to lower taxes. After the election he broke his promise.

If the politician had been honest, he would probably have lost the election.

1. Martin was supposed to graduate from high school in 1995, but he dropped out. He couldn't get a good job after that.

_____

2. Alfred was always faithful to his wife, but last December he found out that she had cheated on him. Alfred divorced his wife last March because of the affair.

_____

3. The students went on strike last week. The government threatened to raise tuition fees. The government would not promise to freeze tuition fees.

_____

4. Carolyn had a pneumonia last month, but she went to work anyway. Last week she was admitted to a hospital, and was forced to get some rest.

_____

5. Yesterday, Santiago ate lunch at an "all you can eat" restaurant. Yesterday afternoon Santiago felt ill, because he had overeaten.

_____

EXERCISE 3

Complete the conditional sentences below. Use the correct tense.

1. If Ellen inherits her father's money, she (invest) it in the stock market. _____

2. If I inherited his money, I (save) it in a term deposit. _____

3. If my late brother had inherited a lot of money, he (spend) it. _____

4. Chris (wait) for you if you had asked him to. _____

5. I (wait) for you if you want me to. _____

6. Probably Jay (wait) for you if he didn't have to pick up his kids. _____

7. My life (be) different if I had married Margaret. _____

8. If you (be) nicer to people, you would have more friends. _____

9. If I (be) nicer to people, I would have had more friends. _____

10. We would have made more progress if we (work) together. _____

11. We would make more progress if we (work) together. _____

12. We will make more progress if we (work) together. _____

Making a Wish

Wish about the Present

We make a wish when we want things to be different. When you wish about a present situation, use the past tense.

> *I wish I **knew** how to play the violin.*
>
> (I can't play the violin, but I would like to.)

With the verb *be*, always use the *were* form.

> *She wishes that she **were** thinner.*

Wish about the Past

When you wish you could change a past situation, use the past perfect tense.

> *Yukio wishes that he **had told** the truth to his wife.*

Wish ⟶ past perfect tense

EXERCISE 4

Write the correct form of the verb in parentheses.

1. I wish I (stay) _____ in school when I was young. I'm 38, and I work in a restaurant. It's not a terrible job, but the salary is very low. If I (stay) _____ in school when I was a teenager, maybe I would have had an easier life. I wish I (think) _____ more about my future when I was a teenager.

2. Diego wishes he (understand) _____ English. He speaks Spanish, but he can't really communicate very well in English. He wishes that he (have) _____ the time to take a language course, but he can't because he works long hours.

3. Heather wishes that she (go) _____ to the show last night. She didn't come with us, and now she knows that the show was really fantastic.

4. Barry wishes that he (break up, not) _____ with his girlfriend last month. Now his girlfriend is dating someone else, and Barry misses her. He wishes that he (try) _____ harder to keep the relationship going. Now Barry feels lonely and he wishes that he (have) _____ a new girlfriend.

Conditionals Review

Possible Future: If & present tense ——————→ future tense

Unlikely Present: If & past tense ——————→ would* (go, eat …)
                   were ————————→

Impossible Past: If & past perfect tense ——————→ would have (past participle)

Wish About the Present: Wish ——————→ past tense
                    ————————→ were

Wish About the Past: Wish ——————→ past perfect tense

Could, expressing possibility, can be used instead of *would*, which expresses intention.

CLASS EXERCISE: REVIEW

Complete the sentences below. Remember to use the correct tense.

1. If you (give) _____ me your telephone number, I will call you, and if I have the time later, I (visit) _____ you.

2. If Anna had a million dollars, she (spend) _____ the money in Las Vegas. She loves to go there. I hate gambling. If I had a million dollars, I (invest) _____ in real estate. I (buy) _____ a piece of land in the interior of British Columbia.

3. If you (see) _____ Rosa, will you tell her that I called. I really need to talk with her. I want to apologize to her. Yesterday, I was really rude to her. I wish I (be) _____ nicer to Rosa yesterday. If I (stop) _____ to think about her feelings, instead of just mouthing off, I would have realized that she was really upset by my comments.

4. Rick is so lazy. He never studies; he just spends hours playing video games. He failed his math test yesterday. If he (study) _____ , he (pass) _____ the test, but he didn't study at all. I keep telling Rick, "If you study, you (pass) _____ your tests!" I wish that Rick (listen) _____ to me more often.

5. I wish my mother (go) _____ to the dentist last year. Instead, she waited until her pain was unbearable, and yesterday she had an expensive root canal. If she (go) _____ to the dentist sooner, she could have avoided the costly procedure.

 # Combining and Punctuating Sentences

When you write in English now, it is important to use a variety of sentence types. Essays written entirely with simple sentences are fine when you are a beginning student in English, but now it is important to use more complex sentences. In the first part of this section, you will practice combining simple sentences to create more complex and interesting sentences.

Combining Sentences

Sentence Types

A *simple* sentence has one independent clause, or one complete idea.

> *The local team won the field hockey game.*

A *compound* sentence contains two or more complete ideas joined by a coordinating conjunction. You know a sentence is compound when you can cover the coordinating conjunction (*and, but, or, nor, for*) and still have two complete sentences.

> *Some apples were full of worms this season, **but** the strawberries were perfectly formed.*

A *complex* sentence contains one independent clause (complete idea) and one dependent clause (incomplete idea).

> dependent clause   independent clause
>
> ***Although some apples were full of worms**, I still refuse to spray the trees with pesticides.*

Although some apples were full of worms cannot stand alone even though it has a subject and a verb. The subordinator *although* turns this into a fragment, or part, of another sentence. Some other subordinators are *who, what, when, where, why, that, which, unless, because, in spite of, until.*

CLASS EXERCISE

A. On a piece of paper, practice making one compound sentence and one complex sentence out each group of sentences.

B. Combine each group of sentences into a single sentence.

Example: (A) Last night I was very tired **but** I watched a program anyway. (compound)

I watched a program **that was on the CBC**. (complex)

1. a. Last night, I was very tired.
   b. I watched a program anyway.
   c. The program was called *Witness*.
   d. It was on the CBC.
   e. It was about Japan.
   f. The Japanese are interested in Canada.

2. a. There is a theme park in Japan.
   b. The park is called "Canada Land."
   c. There is an *Anne of Green Gables* exhibit in Canada Land.
   d. There is a replica of a Quebec City street in Canada Land.
   e. There are not exhibits about every part of Canada.

Sentence Hints

Combining sentences to make a clear sentence is not too difficult if you can avoid the following pitfalls:

1. Use *who* or *whom* to begin a clause only when you are adding information about a **person**.

   *The young children, **whom I'd never seen before**, were making a lot of noise.*

2. When you are giving further information about a **place** or **thing**, use *which* or *that*.

   *The series of articles **that I'm working on** should be ready soon.*

   *The items **which were stolen** were in my purse.*

3. When you use interrupting phrases in a sentence, make sure that your subject still agrees with your verb.

   *The **Fringe Festival**, which is located in Edmonton, **attracts** a lot of entertainers.*

EXERCISE 1

Combine the sentences with *who* or *that*. Sentences may be structured in more than one way.

1. _____

Maxine is an only child. She is very spoiled.

2. _____

The issues must be resolved. We discussed those issues.

3. _____

Long division can be very important. You learned long division in high school.

4. _____

Susan lives next door. She is a single mother.

5. _____

The plates are on the table. My grandmother gave me those plates.

Where in a clause is used to give more information about a place.

> The house is old and quaint. Kramer lives in the house.
>
> The house **where Kramer lives** is old and quaint.

Whose is used to indicate possession. It can replace *his*, *her*, *its* or *their*.

> I saw a dog. Its collar was missing.
>
> I saw a dog **whose collar was missing.**

EXERCISE 2

Combine the sentences. Use *where* or *whose*.

> Example: Did you see the two women. ~~Their~~ (whose) dresses were identical.

1. The restaurant is understaffed. We ate in that restaurant this morning.

_____

2. Ralph saw a young, shy girl. Her date was very tall.

_____

3. That is the safe. I keep my valuables in that safe.

_____

4. The hospital has burned down. Kelly was born in that hospital.

_____

5. Did you notice that man? His tie is on crooked.

_____

6. The garage is expensive. My car was repaired in that garage.

_____

Sentence Construction Problems

Fragments and run-ons are two common errors students make when combining sentences.

A *fragment* is an incomplete sentence. Make sure that your sentence contains a complete thought.

Fragment: *Because I really needed to see him.*

Correct: *I was upset because I really needed to see him.*

A *run-on* occurs when two or more complete sentences are incorrectly connected.

Run-on: *Maria missed the bus to work, she was extremely late.*

The above sentence could be corrected in the following ways:

1. Create two complete sentences   *Maria missed the bus to work. She was extremely late.*

2. Add a subordinator   ***Because*** *Maria missed the bus to work, she was extremely late.*

3. Add a coordinator   *Maria missed the bus to work* **and** *she was extremely late.*

4. Add a semicolon (;)   *Maria missed the bus to work; she was extremely late.*

EXERCISE 3

Identify all correct sentences with *C*. Write *F* beside fragments, and *RO* beside run-ons.

1. First, the best way to discipline children.

2. I think that children should not be hit. _____

3. That is a controversial topic, many talk shows discuss that issue. _____

4. I think that children can learn to distinguish right from wrong with a lecture, some disagree. _____

5. Because small children won't always understand explanations. _____

6. Some people believe that small children should be spanked if they do something wrong. _____

7. Small children understand that they are being bad when parents speak in a loud voice. _____

8. But not everyone can be convinced of that. _____

EXERCISE 4

Complete the dialogue by putting one of the following transition words in the spaces provided.

however	as soon as	therefore
although	as long as	furthermore
because	in spite of	besides

Dear Edwin,

(1) _____ I haven't written to you for quite some time, I have been thinking of you. (2) _____ I have some free time, I will come by your office and invite you for a drink. (3) _____ of my extremely busy workload, (4) _____ , I don't foresee having any extra time until next month. (5) _____ our busy schedules, we really should keep in touch more regularly. If we let our friends disappear, what will we do when we're old and retired?

I want to fill you in on my activities these days. The private eye business is going full steam. Right now I'm working on cases that require a lot of skill and patience. (6) _____ I can't tell you the details, I can give you some broad outlines of the cases I'm working on. Of course, I've got the requisite number of cheating spouse cases, but the most interesting investigation I'm doing is for a mysterious, beautiful lady. She comes in here and, (7) _____ the NO SMOKING signs everywhere, she smokes constantly, lighting one cigarette from the burning butt of another. She puts them out in a portable ashtray that she carries in her purse. (8) _____ , she drinks cup after cup from my espresso machine, yet (9) _____ all that stimulation, she talks with a slow, languid drawl, and moves with the laziness of a cat. I don't say a word about the smoking because she's too interesting to insult; (10) _____ , she's paying me a small fortune.

I can't say any more about this. I really have got a lot of work to do. Take care of yourself, and drop me a line.

Sincerely,

James Jameson

EXERCISE 5

Combine the following sentences into a single sentence. There may be more than one correct answer.

Malcolm entered the hotel room.

He put his briefcase on the desk.

Malcolm wanted to open his briefcase.

The briefcase was locked.

Malcolm didn't remember the combination for the lock.

Malcolm opened the case anyway.

He smashed the lock with a small hammer.

_____

_____

_____

_____

Punctuating Sentences

You have practiced combining sentences. Notice that there can be punctuation problems when you write longer sentences. Sentences that are incorrectly joined together can become run-on sentences. This part of Chapter 9 contains explanations for the proper use of the comma and the semicolon in English.

English as a Second Language students may also encounter problems with capitalizing. For example, days of the week are not capitalized in many Latin languages, but they are always capitalized in English.

Do the following exercises carefully so that you can learn to eliminate capitalization and sentence punctuation problems.

Capitalization

When to Use Capitals

Always capitalize the following:

1. The pronoun *I*.

2. The days of the week, the months, and holidays.

   Tuesday   *May 22*   *Labour Day*

When to Use Capitals

3. The names of specific places, such as buildings, streets, parks, public squares, lakes, rivers, cities, provinces, and countries.

Elm Street	*Lake Louise*	*Regina, Saskatchewan*
Jarry Park	*St. Lawrence River*	*California*
Times Square	*Austria*	*Dylan Elementary School*

4. The names of languages, nationalities, tribes, races, and religions.

Norwegian	*Mohawk*	*Catholic*

5. The titles of specific individuals.

General Audet	*the Senator*	*Doctor Mortis*

    If you are referring to the profession in general, do not use capitals.

a general	*senators*	*the doctors*

6. The major words in titles.

The Catcher in the Rye	*The Diviners*	*War and Peace*

EXERCISE 6

Add capitals, where needed, to the following sentences.

1. next monday we hope to visit castle mountain in banff national park, and in july we will go down the elbow river on an inner tube.

2. we asked the colonel if he was aware of the problems in the military, but he claimed that the sergeants hadn't told him a thing.

3. in ireland the catholics and the protestants have been fighting for over a century.

4. many presidents of major companies listened to president goldsmith's speech.

5. students at churchill high school can study latin, german and spanish as well as french, but other high school students in the area cannot.

Punctuating Titles

Place the title of a short work (song, essay, poem, short story, article from a magazine or newspaper) in quotation marks. (" ")

> My brother used to listen to "Stairway to Heaven" every evening.

Underline the title of a longer work (book, TV show, play, movie, newspaper, magazine, or work of art) or use italics if you are typing a document.

> Last summer, when we were in London, we saw the play <u>Evita</u>.

CLASS EXERCISE

Add capitals, where needed, to the following sentences, and properly punctuate titles. The first word of each sentence is already capitalized.

In may, my friend rita and i read east of eden. We are both avid readers, but she prefers reading short stories whereas I like long novels. Her favorite short story is called bugs, by nancy holmes. She also likes to go to the theater, and she enjoys reading plays. She wants me to read the play murder in the cathedral, by t.s. eliot. She said that the play takes place in a place called canterbury.

At the moment we are sitting by a river drinking a glass of iced tea and reading. The st. lawrence river is rushing by, and lake of two mountains isn't very far from here. I have a magazine with me today. I am going to read the article how to communicate in relationships, by doctor nancy wilder. I started to read the article on wednesday, but i haven't had time to finish it. Today rita just has a copy of the montreal gazette.

Using the Comma and the Semicolon

When to Use the Comma

Some uses of the comma are:

1. to separate items in a series of nouns, adverbs, verbs, or phrases. (A series = more than two.) The use of a comma before the final "and" or "or" is optional.
    We were impressed with her poise, her simplicity, and her kindness.
    They shouldn't leave at this moment, in a day or even in a week.

2. to set off phrases that give additional information about the noun.
    Mr. Green, the man in the yellow trenchcoat, is a secret agent.

3. to set off introductory phrases such as *by the way, on the other hand, in the first place.*
    On the other hand, we could cancel the meeting.

4. to signal that an introductory clause has ended. A clause is "introductory" if it begins with a subordinator (see list below).
    *She worked very hard **in spite of** her poor health.* (No comma)
    ***In spite of** her poor health, she worked very hard.* (Comma)

Subordinators

Time clause	as soon as, as long as, when, whenever, while, since, until
Unexpected result	although, even though, despite, in spite of
Opposite clause	whereas
Clause of reason	because, due to, so, since (meaning "because"), as (meaning "because")

EXERCISE 7

When necessary, add commas to the following sentences.

1. Due to the poor visibility driving on the highway is not recommended.

2. You should know my friend that I have remarried my first wife.

3. We bought medical supplies including Band-Aids gauze peroxide antibacterial gel and tape.

4. I will jog every morning as long as I am able to.

5. Until you get a raise we should curb our spending.

When to Use the Semicolon

Use a semicolon:

1. when two sentences with complete ideas are joined together.

I think that bank machines are a necessity; my uncle refuses to use them.

2. when the second independent clause is introduced with a transitional expression like *therefore, however, furthermore, moreover, in fact* or *nevertheless*. Put a semicolon before, and a comma after, these transitional expressions when they introduce the second complete idea.

I showed my uncle how to use bank machines; nevertheless, he refuses to use them.

Our estimate for the work was very low; however, another company's bid was lower.

EXERCISE 8

Read the following sentences and correct any errors in punctuation, subject-verb agreement, or use of *who* and *that*.

Example: History is a subject who I adore. *"Who" is incorrect and should be replaced by "that."*

1. Young people who commits murder should be tried as adults.

2. Although I had never discussed the issue with my husband. I knew that he would support my decision.

3. Most humans believe in life after death, they want to believe that life has meaning.

4. The hockey league is a business who has been changed by million dollar salaries.

5. My teacher Mr. Steinberg loves to tell us stories about his youth.

6. Somebody removed the old suitcases that was under the bed.

7. Last month I read a really good article who said that ghosts exist.

8. Sales have fallen drastically, furthermore the company is in danger of becoming bankrupt.

9. That man, who is very nosey, always discuss my problems.

10. The game was canceled. Because of the bad weather.

CLASS EXERCISE

Read the following sentences and correct any errors in capitalization, punctuation, subject-verb agreement, or use of *who* and *that*.

1. *The White Hotel* is a novel who is greatly admired.

2. Although the story was very sad it was quite entertaining.

3. At that moment, Morgan and Alexandra, who was Arthur's half sisters, disappeared into thin air.

4. The police found the weapon who killed the old man.

5. The extinction of the dodo bird is a subject that interest me very much.

6. My cousin Arnie thinks that our grandmother is a nasty old lady, I think that granny is a sweetheart.

7. There are some interesting exhibits at the museum; and the entrance fee is very reasonable.

8. His new novel about some spies who evaded capture have become a bestseller.

9. Last week I saw a fantastic movie called voyage of the damned, it was about a terrible tragedy.

10. Because I am so busy I don't have time to work on that project with you.

11. The children don't have any winter boots, furthermore, we have run out of money.

12. Martin who is a member of the chess club, never wants to play chess with his younger sister.

13. On Tuesdays, my book-reading group gets together to discuss a novel, now we're discussing the novel, "wide sargasso sea," by Jean Rhys.

14. The Rocky mountains are incredible; and many people think that all tourists should visit them.

15. The Senators had to vote on the new bill, but I know of one Senator, Senator Gerard, who will vote against it.

10 Quotes and Reported Speech

Whenever you quote a passage, or even paraphrase an author's thoughts, it is extremely important to credit the author whose ideas you are using. Never present the words of someone else as if they were your own, or you could be accused of plagiarism.

When you write a formal paper containing a bibliography, you should refer to MLA rules for citing references. In more informal opinion essays, you do not need to include a bibliography, but it is extremely important to acknowledge the source of any material that you borrow.

Introducing and Punctuating a Quote

1. In informal essays, refer to the author and title in the sentence introducing or following the quote. After a complete introductory sentence, use a colon (:) followed by quotation marks (" ").

   Dorothy Nixon, in her essay "The Appalling Truth," describes the effect of the telephone on modern humans: "The telephone has made us slaves, in the Pavlovian sense, to a ringing bell."

2. After an introductory phrase, use a comma followed by quotation marks.

   In her essay "The Appalling Truth," Dorothy Nixon says, "The telephone has made us slaves, in the Pavlovian sense, to a ringing bell."

3. If the quote isn't a complete sentence but is integrated into your own sentence, no punctuation other than quotation marks is necessary.

   Dorothy Nixon, in her essay "The Appalling Truth," claims that our phones have turned us into "slaves, in the Pavlovian sense, to a ringing bell."

4. The end punctuation of a quote is always placed inside the quotation marks.

   "What are you doing?" she asked.

   "The snails are superb!" he announced.

5. If the end of the quote isn't the end of your sentence, end the quote with a comma instead of a period.

   "With the invention of the clock we have lost the ability to live in the present," according to Dorothy Nixon.

6. Quotes of more than three lines in length should be indented and single spaced, and no quotation marks are necessary.

7. If you are quoting dialogue, begin a new paragraph each time the speaker changes.

EXERCISE 1

Punctuate the following sentences.

1. We really ought to leave now Rita muttered before he returns

2. Diego Parrera in his article in Sports Illustrated says An athlete is only as good as his or her last performance

3. Does anyone want to join me Tracy asked

4. According to Samuel Cleaver in his song An Odious Message the extinction of the dinosaurs contains a message for humans Who will study our bones when they end up in sandstone

5. Those convicted of drunk driving should lose their license for at least five years Marvin insisted.

   Gaby said That's a little harsh.

   That's because your father wasn't killed by a drunk driver Marvin responded loudly.

6. Various novels including The Catcher in the Rye are taught in high schools throughout North America.

Reported Speech

If you are a reporter working for a newspaper or magazine, you must report what someone said. Most newspaper articles do not contain a lot of direct quotes, but state what someone said indirectly. For example, a reporter might write: *The finance minister said that new ways must be found to reduce the deficit. He asked all of us to be partners in the government's new deficit-reducing schemes.*

Although it is interesting and useful to quote respected sources when you are writing an essay, it is also important to know how to properly report what reliable sources said. Notice the verb changes that occur when spoken words become reported words.

When we report a conversation after the fact, this is called *reported speech*. Because we are describing the conversation after it occurred, the past forms of verbs are generally used.

Quote   Reported Speech

Sara said, "I'm very busy."   *She said that she **was** very busy.*

Most verbs change to the past tense.

am / is ——————→ *was*   have ——————→ *had*

are   ——————→ *were*   do   ——————→ *did*

Change some modals in reported speech.

will ——————→ *would*

can   ——————→ *could*

may   ——————→ *might*

All other modals remain the same (*would, could, might, should, must, ought to*).

John: I should get ready for work.   *He said that he should get ready for work.*

The simple past can usually stay the same in reported speech, or you can change it to the past perfect.

Michele said, "I lost my keys." ——————→ *Michele said that she **lost** her keys.*
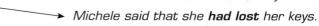
                                          *Michele said that she **had lost** her keys.*

EXERCISE 2

Last Saturday you overheard this conversation. Report what was said by changing the following quotes to reported speech.

Quote   Reported Speech

Example: Roy: Tom is going to leave   Roy said (that) *Tom was going to leave*
his wife.   *his wife.*

1. Ann: Tom's wife will be devastated!   Ann said _____

_____

2. Roy: I know that.   Roy said _____

_____

3. Ann: Tom is a two-timer!   Ann said _____

_____

4. Roy: Tom is having a midlife crisis.   Roy said _____

_____

5. Ann: I can talk to Tom about it.

Ann said _____

6. Roy: No, I will talk to him.

Roy said _____

_____

Other words change in reported speech.

Quote	Reported Speech
this	*that*
these	*those*
today	*that day*
now	*then*

EXERCISE 3

This dialogue was originally on the radio twenty years ago. Change the dialogue to reported speech.

Jay: I have an amazing new product. It is a hair restorer called Hair-In! Even if a man is completely bald, this product will restore some of his hair. Hair-In is made of rare plants from China. Many men will attest to the power of this product. If any listener is bald, and this product doesn't satisfy him, the money will be refunded. Hair-In costs only two dollars.

Jay said that he had an amazing new product. He said ... _____

_____

_____

_____

_____

When to Use Say and Tell

Use *say*:

1. in direct quotations.

*Dimitrius **said**, "I am going to bed."*

2. in indirect (reported) quotations.

*Dimitrius **said** that he was going to bed.*
(*that* is optional)

Use *tell*:

1. when you give a message to somebody.

*Dimitrius **told me** that he was going to bed. Did he **tell you** that too?*

2. with the expressions *tell a lie, tell the truth, tell a secret.*

EXERCISE 4

Write *say* or *tell* in the spaces provided.

1. Last night Calvin _____ that he was going to bed but he really _____ a lie.

2. His parents _____ him to turn out his light and go to sleep.

3. They _____ that Calvin had been grumpy all day and they _____ that Calvin needed a good night's sleep.

4. Calvin _____ his parents that he would obey them, but instead he grabbed a book and a flashlight and he read under the covers.

5. In the morning, Calvin's parents _____ that he looked very tired.

6. Calvin _____ his parents that he had had a very bad dream.

7. When Calvin's mother _____ that she knew he had been reading during the night, Calvin _____ the truth to his parents.

Some terms can give a better indication of how something was stated than the word *said*.

state	*mention*	*announce*	*offer*
comment	*reply*	*warn*	*remark*
assure	*insist*	*explain*	*admit*

Compare: *Alex **said** that he had made a mistake.*

*Calvin **admitted** that he had made a mistake.*

CLASS EXERCISE

Look again at the text about Calvin. Try to replace *say* with any of the terms in the list above. (There are many possible choices.)

Reported Speech: Questions Form

You don't need to preserve the special question word order when the question is inside another, so the auxiliary after the question word is no longer necessary. However, you do need to change the present tense to the *past* tense.

Auxiliary

What **do** you think about it?   *She asked me what I thought about it.*

If there is no question word, use *if* or *whether* to introduce the "inside" question.

Is it cold?   *He asked if it was cold.*

He asked whether it was cold.

EXERCISE 5

Report what the customs inspector asked you yesterday.

Quote	Reported Speech
1. What is your name?	She asked me *what my name was.*
2. How are you?	She asked me
3. Do you have any alcohol or cigarettes?	She asked me
4. How long are you going to stay in Canada?	She asked me
5. Do you have any food in your bag?	She asked me
6. What gifts are you carrying?	She asked me
7. When will you leave the country?	She asked me
8. Can you open that bag please?	She asked me
9. Would you please follow that inspector?	She asked me
10. Do you have anything to declare?	She asked me

CLASS EXERCISE

Read the following conversation and then report what was said. Use the word in parentheses.

1. "I need some help," Jack said. (announce)

2. "A wolf is trying to eat me," Jack said. (explain)

3. "I see no wolf around here!" Mr. Ranger said. (comment)

4. "There really is no wolf. I just wanted to see someone," Jack said. (admit)

5. "Now I won't listen to any of your cries for help," Mr. Ranger said. (warn)

6. "I promise that I won't lie again!" Jack said. (assure)

Review of Sections 6 to 10

CLASS EXERCISE A: PLURALS REVIEW

Add *s* to all nouns that require the plural form. For irregular plurals, rewrite the noun.

(1) My ideal man is a man who is sensitive, caring, witty, and clever. He has black hair and deep blue eye. He has cute foot and a nice behind. I'm really kidding about these physical aspect, though.

(2) Really, my ideal man is someone who cares a lot about his parent. I don't like man who are disrespectful to their elder.

(3) Finally, my ideal man is someone that most person like. If one of my friend hates this man, then he definitely isn't ideal!

CLASS EXERCISE B: MODALS REVIEW

Find and correct the modal errors in the following sentences. If the sentence is correct, write *C* in the space provided.

1. _____ I firmly believe that the age for getting a driver's license should be raise to eighteen.

2. _____ Many accidents could be avoid if only the young driver had more experience.

3. _____ Why he has to find a job?

4. _____ Mark should has known not to put the empty milk carton in the fridge!

5. _____ Sally shouldn't complain about her co-workers so much!

6. _____ When does the new law should be imposed?

7. _____ We think that the law should be implement as soon as possible.

8. _____ When you can help us to make the cookies?

9. _____ Where Margaret and I should meet you?

10. _____ Yesterday I shouldn't had worked late because I missed my daughter's dance recital.

CLASS EXERCISE C: CONDITIONALS REVIEW

Complete the conditional sentences below.

If I can, I (give up) _____ smoking. I wish I (know) _____ how to stop. I am pregnant, and I know that my smoking could hurt my baby, but I'm totally addicted to cigarettes. I wish that I (never, start) _____ smoking. I was so foolish. When I was 14, I just tried smoking because I wanted to see what it felt like. If I hadn't bummed cigarettes off of my friends, maybe I (become, not) _____ addicted. If I (know) _____ , when I was 14, how hard it is to quit smoking, maybe I (never, take) _____ that first puff.

CLASS EXERCISE D: PUNCTUATING SENTENCES REVIEW

Add proper punctuation and capitalization to the following sentences.

1. I don't have any particular religious belief moreover i don't think i'll ever be religious even though my parents are devout catholics.

2. Every sunday morning i sit at home reading the calgary herald newspaper i only go to church during the months of december and april.

3. I read an interesting article in the magazine called natural science the article was called the human need for religious beliefs.

4. The article was written by a professor i think his name is professor santoni.

5. Because of the human need to believe that life has meaning virtually all cultures on earth consider that there is some type of existence after death.

6. Next to some neanderthal skulls near the basin of the kroll river evidence of a burial site was found stones were placed in a circle.

7. On the other hand the stone circle could have no significance in fact the stones could have been placed near the skulls at a later date.

8. Although his colleagues disagree one individual professor santoni thinks that even some apes have death rituals.

CLASS EXERCISE E: REPORTED SPEECH REVIEW

Change the quotes to reported speech.

	Quote	Reported Speech
1.	Could someone help me?	He asked if *someone could help him*
2.	Does anyone have the time?	He asked if
3.	Someone is at the door.	He mentioned that
4.	Can someone answer the door?	He asked if
5.	The neighbor needs some sugar.	He stated that
6.	There is no sugar left.	I replied that
7.	Will you buy some later?	He asked me if
8.	I won't have time to do it.	I answered that
9.	Does the corner store sell sugar?	He asked me if
10.	I can go to the store after lunch.	He explained that

CLASS EXERCISE F: QUOTATION MARKS REVIEW

Add quotation marks to the following text, or underline titles, when necessary.

Tracy Winland is a very efficient book editor. At the moment she is editing the cookbook One Hundred Chocolate Recipes. One summer morning she headed out for her usual coffee break.

Does anyone want to join me? she asked her co-workers.

No one did, so she went down the elevator to the ground floor of the building, and stopped at Lee's Newsstand, as usual.

A newspaper and a Boffo Chocobar please, she said. Tracy loves Boffo brand chocolate bars.

You really don't need to say a thing, Mr. Lee replied. I know that you always buy a newspaper and a Boffo Chocobar!

Once outside, Tracy sat on a long low wall. She was busy reading the article Health Matters in the Montreal Gazette when a handsome young man wearing a canary-yellow shirt sat on the wall next to her. The man was whistling the tune Over the Rainbow, and tucked under his elbow was a copy of Computer Magazine.

While Tracy was reading her article, the young man reached for the Boffo Chocobar on the ledge between them, broke off a large piece, and ate it. Tracy stared at the stranger. He hadn't even asked for a bite! Are you enjoying that? she inquired.

Oh yes, the young man replied, I certainly am. It's delicious.

To Tracy's horror the man then grabbed the bar, broke off another large piece, and ate that too. Barely a third of the chocolate bar was left. You've got some nerve, Tracy spit out, glaring into the man's surprised face. I'm going to finish this bar, if you don't mind!

At that, Tracy snatched the bar right out of the man's grasp, and stomped off. Some people are so rude! she called over her shoulder. On her way into the office building she ran into some co-workers, and she immediately told them about the chocolate bar thief. Everyone was very solicitous; they knew how much Tracy loved her chocolate.

As Tracy was walking through the lobby towards the elevator, Mr. Lee called out: Miss Winland! Come and get your Boffo Chocobar. You left it on my counter this morning!

11 Spelling

Because most languages have varieties of rules, and inconsistent pronunciation, spelling errors can and do occur. Even native English speakers make spelling mistakes.

Most of us have certain bad spelling habits. For example, some students constantly misspell the word *which* by writing *wich*. The best way to break a bad spelling habit is to keep a list of such spelling errors. Then, after you write a text, always reread your text specifically for spelling errors and consult your list to check that your habitual errors have not reoccurred. It is also very important to have a dictionary handy when you do a writing assignment.

If you are proficient on the computer, then you know that most computer programs have a spellcheck function. Be careful, however. Spellchecks can find some misspelled words, but not words that sound alike but differ in meaning. For example, a spellcheck would not find the mistakes in this sentence: *Your to late for the meeting at there house.*

EXERCISE 1

The following words are incorrectly spelled. Write down each word correctly.

Example:

tomorow   *tomorrow*

1.	familly	_____	**6.**	embarassed	_____
2.	bussiness	_____	**7.**	sollution	_____
3.	scool	_____	**8.**	laught	_____
4.	writting	_____	**9.**	beggining	_____
5.	happenning	_____	**10.**	writting	_____

CLASS EXERCISE

In the space provided: Write "f" if the *gh* sounds like *f*
Write "t" if the *ght* sounds like *t*
Write "silent" if the *gh* is silent.

1. rough _____

2. taught _____

3. borough _____

4. thought _____

5. laugh _____

6. thorough _____

7. brought _____

8. cough _____

9. although _____

10. slaughter _____

Spelling Tip 1: *Whose and Who's*

Whose indicates possession and replaces *his, her, its* or *their*.
Who's is the contracted form of *who is*.

EXERCISE 2

Choose the correct words from the lists provided.

1. (*his / is / has / as*)

_____ that Tom's desk? I need to leave this package on _____ desk. _____ he in the building? _____ anyone seen him? _____ soon _____ he arrives, could someone let me know? _____ anyone listening to me?

2. (*whose / who's / live / leave*)

_____ cat is that? That cat's meowing is disturbing me! _____ going to do something about it? Does that cat _____ with someone? How can I make the cat _____ this room?

3. (*your / you're*)

Is that _____ pen? I need to sign that letter. If _____ not using that pen right now, could I borrow it, please?

4. (*their / there / they're*)

_____ are many people in this country who can't find work. I have two unemployed uncles. _____ trying very hard to find jobs but _____ are no jobs available. Both uncles have lost _____ cars, and now they may lose _____ homes because they can no longer pay the mortgages.

5. (*to / too / two*)

There are _____ reasons for me to stay at my job. There are perhaps several reasons why I should leave, _____ . If I go _____ another workplace, I may find myself with the same types of problems. It's really _____ difficult to make a decision now.

6. (*advise / advice*)

My sister Carol came to me for some _____ . She was thinking of entering an art program at the local university, instead of entering nursing. Unfortunately, I wasn't sure how to _____ her. If I suggested that she pursue art, maybe she wouldn't like my _____ , and if I suggested that she take the safer route and study nursing, maybe she would just ignore my _____ and study art anyway.

EXERCISE 3

These sentences each have one spelling mistake. Circle the spelling error in each sentence and write the word correctly in the space provided.

1. My father always gives me good advise. _____

2. Anne has been living alone for to long. _____

3. That wonderful new stereo over their is mine! _____

4. When my fly was open it was really embarassing. _____

5. Could you please ask John if he as seen Andy? _____

6. I though about it, but I don't want to do it. _____

7 I can't help you because I still have to much work to do. _____

8. Whose going to help me carry these boxes? _____

9. That is the man who's wife is in jail. _____

10. It is difficult to understand there reaction. _____

11. Martin is the type of person whose concerned about others. _____

12. Please do the work whit me. _____

13. I will make a thorough review of your case. _____

14. I would like to order an other coffee please. _____

15. The mariage of Sam and Rita will take place next Sunday. _____

EXERCISE 4

Spelling Tip 2: *IE* and *EI*

The following rhyme can help you remember when to write *ie* and when to write *ei*.
I before *E*, except after *C*, or when sounding like "ay" as in *neighbor* and *weigh*.

Which word is correctly spelled? Put A, B or C in the space provided.

1. A. deseive   B. deceive   C. decieve   _____
2. A. responsabillity B. responsability   C. responsibility   _____
3. A. receive   B. recieve   C. resieve   _____
4. A. proove   B. prouve   C. prove   _____
5. A. exaggerate   B. exagerrate   C. exagerate   _____
6. A. believe   B. beleive   C. believ   _____
7. A. suceed   B. succede   C. succeed   _____
8. A. reciept   B. receipt   C. reseipt   _____
9. A. liscence   B. lisense   C. license   _____
10. A. freight train   B. frieght train   C. frate train   _____

EXERCISE 5

Choose the correct words from the list provided.

1. (*lose / loose / lost*)

    I didn't _____ my snake ring. I gave it to my sister because it was too _____ for me. Unfortunately, I _____ my wedding ring at the mall.

2. (*we're / wear / where*)

    _____ is Julie? _____ waiting for her. What does she want to _____ to the show?

3. (*proof / prove*)

    I have no _____ that he committed the crime. Do you have any _____ ? Maybe no one can _____ it.

4. (*choose / choice / chose*)

    What dress are you going to _____ for the wedding? Last week I _____ my dress, but I haven't paid for it yet. This store is great. It is difficult to make a _____ when there are so many dresses to _____ from.

5. (*then / than*)

I think that you are taller _____ I am, but _____ you would be, wouldn't you. You're much older _____ I am.

6. (*whether / weather / dessert / desert*)

I don't know _____ or not you are interested, but it is extremely hot outside. I can't stand this type of _____. I feel like we are living in the middle of the Gobi _____. Maybe I should have something cold, like a big bowl of ice cream, to cool off. I always like to eat _____ after supper.

Spelling Tip 3: Adding a Prefix or a Suffix

When you add a prefix (*un, pre, il,* etc.) to a word, keep the last letter of the prefix and the first letter of the base word.

*un + necessary = un**n**ecessary* (two *n*'s)

The same rule applies to the addition of a suffix. If you add *ly* to a word that ends in *l,* then your new word will have double *l.*

final + ly = *fina**ll**y* (two *l*'s)

CLASS EXERCISE

These sentences each have one spelling mistake. Circle the mistake and write it correctly in the space provided.

1. Sherlock prooved that the butler murdered Mr. Lin. _____

2. I mispelled that word on my test. _____

3. I believe that there is an other way to solve the problem. _____

4. The banks are realy raising the service charges a lot this year. _____

5. I thing that handguns should not be sold. _____

6. Those are the books wich I want to borrow. _____

7. Drug smuggling is an ilegal activity. _____

8. You are acting in a very iresponsible way. _____

9. I didn't expect to like snails but actualy I enjoy them. _____

10. That is an iregular triangle. _____

11. Surelly you don't expect me to clean up that mess! _____

12. My teacher tought us to spell correctly. _____

12 Gallicisms

The English language of today has been influenced by many languages such as German, French, Greek, and the Scandinavian languages. The 11th-century invasion of Britain by the Norman French significantly transformed the English language. Because French was the language of British aristocracy and royalty for the next three centuries, French words permeated the English language, especially in the realms of law, finance, war, and royalty.

Because of the similarities in English and French, mistakes are easy to make. Some words sound the same but are spelled differently. Mistakes also occur when words look the same in both languages, but have completely different meanings.

EXERCISE 1

Write the English equivalent of each of the following French words. These words have the same meaning in both languages, but are spelled differently.

1. adresse _____

2. appartement _____

3. canadien _____

4. caractère _____

5. compagnie _____

6. consécutif _____

7. équipement _____

8. exemple _____

9. futur _____

10. gouvernement _____

11. juge _____

12. humain _____

13. langage _____

14. littérature _____

15. personnalité _____

16. potentiel _____

17. prouve _____

18. responsabilité _____

19. recommandation _____

20. texte _____

CLASS EXERCISE

The following English terms look like French words, but they do not have the same meaning in both languages. To verify that you understand what the following words mean in English, write an English synonym, or brief definition, for each term.

1a. actually _____

1b. presently _____

2a. sensible _____

2b. sensitive _____

3a. animator _____

3b. host _____

4a. formation _____

4b. background _____

5a. deception _____

5b. disappointment _____

6a. win _____

6b. earn _____

7a. vacancy _____

7b. vacation _____

8a. assist _____

8b. attend _____

EXERCISE 2

Sometimes French words or expressions are incorrectly translated. Correct the italicized word or phrase in each of the following sentences.

1. Alana was in a car accident, but don't worry. She is *correct*. _____

2. Arthur is addicted to the television. He *listens* the television every evening. _____

3. Your father thinks you should stay in school and I *am agree* with him. _____

4. Could you please *explain me* why I have to go to bed so early? _____

5. My mother was very *deceived* when I told her that I had failed my test. _____

6. Claude is the *animator* of a new television show. He interviews the guests. _____

7. Ron wants to quit his job because he only *wins* the minimum wage. _____

8. Marie *quit* her boyfriend because he was cheating on her. _____

9. Many terrible things have *arrived* since I last saw you. _____

10. Could you please *open* the radio? I want to listen to some music. _____

EXERCISE 3

Correct the translation error in each of the following sentences. (The incorrect word is in italics.)

1. Carl Sagan is a well-known *scientifique*, and he is the author of the book *Cosmos*. _____

2. Marie-Claire is going to do her teaching *stage* at the new high school.

_____

3. Dr. Peablo has done some extremely interesting psychological *experiences*.

_____

4. Terry has a *formation* in physics, but he is currently working as an astronomy teacher.

_____

5. During my summer *vacancy* I went to Cape Cod, in the United States.

_____

6. I really love Celine Dion, but I have never *assisted at* any of her concerts.

_____

7. That movie is really *humoristic*. I laughed throughout the movie!

_____

8. I like to *pass* my weekends at our cabin by the lake.

_____

CLASS EXERCISE

Correct the translation error in each of the following sentences. (The incorrect word is in italics. The italicized word may have been incorrectly translated, or incorrectly spelled.)

1. I feel really *deceived* because I failed my math test. I really should have studied.

_____

2. My father has two jobs because he doesn't *win* enough money with just one job.

_____

3. Antoine rarely takes *responsability* for his actions.

_____

4. Please *close* the lights when you leave the room.

_____

5. During our summer *vacancy* we went to Newfoundland.

_____

6. *Actually* I'm working as an accountant, but I hope to change jobs soon.

_____

7. Greg has a perfect attendance record. So far this year he has *assisted at* all of his classes.

_____

8. That young boy cries when he hears sad music because he is so *sensible*.

_____

9. The lawyer is trying to *prouve* that his client is innocent.

_____

10. How do you intend to *pass* your summer?

_____

11. I'm sorry, but I can't discuss that with you. It's *personel*.

_____

12. Octavio just got a job as the *animator* of a quiz show.

_____

13. In order to get that job, you need a *formation* in computers.

_____

14. Some people speculate that in the *futur* the middle class will disappear.

_____

15. Martin *quit* work yesterday at midnight, and today he starts at 9 a.m.

_____

Appendix 1

Parts of Speech

Knowing the parts of speech is useful when you need to edit a text. If you can recognize the type of error you may be better able to remember how to correct it.

Parts of Speech

A	the article (*a*, *the*, ...)
N	the noun: a person, place or thing
V	the verb: the action word
Adv	the adverb: adds information about the verb (*typed* **rapidly**)
Adj	the adjective: adds information about the noun (**blue** *sky*)
P	the preposition (*in*, *on*, *at*, ...)
Pro	the pronoun (*I*, *me*, *my*, *mine*, *myself* ...)

CLASS EXERCISE

In the following sentences, identify the parts of speech. Leave blank any part of speech that you cannot identify.

```
     (N)    (V) (Pro) (Adj)    (N)    (P) (Pro)  (N)
Example: Maria  held  her  lovely  rosary  in   her   hand.
```

1. The nanny put the baby in its crib.

2. The blue documents are in the drawer of my desk.

3. The old man held the little dog gingerly.

4. The tiny bug bit the child on the leg.

5. Margaret carefully reads *People* magazine.

6. An efficient reporter asked his boss for a bonus.

7. She gently lifted the tired child.

8. The surprised woman politely thanked her cousin.

Appendix 2

Gerunds and Infinitives

1. Gerunds

A *gerund* is a verb in the *ing* form. Some verbs in English are always followed by a gerund. Do not confuse gerunds with progressive verb forms.
Notice the difference:

Nadia is sewing her dress. ⟶ *Sewing* is in the present progressive form. Nadia is in the process of doing something.

*Frank finished **sewing** his pants.* ⟶ *Sewing* is a gerund that follows *finish*. After *finish*, you must use a gerund. You cannot write "Frank finished to sew his pants."

Some Common Verbs Followed by Gerunds

appreciate	enjoy	quit
avoid	finish	recall
complete	involve	recollect
consider	keep	regret
delay	mention	remember
deny	mind	resent
discuss	miss	resist
dislike	postpone	risk
practice	stop	

Gerunds are also used after the expressions *to be worth* and *no use*.

2. Infinitives

An *infinitive* is a verb in the *to* form. Some verbs in English are followed by the infinitive.

*We can't afford **to buy** a new car.* ——→ After the word *afford* you must use the infinitive form. You cannot say "We can't afford buying a new car."

Some Common Verbs Followed by Infinitives			
afford	demand	mean	seem
agree	deserve	need	threaten
appear	expect	prepare	volunteer
arrange	fail	pretend	want
ask	hesitate	promise	wish
claim	hope	refuse	would like
consent	learn	regret	struggle
decide	manage	plan	swear

3. Gerunds or Infinitives

Some verbs can be followed by either a gerund or an infinitive, and keep the same meaning.

*Martin loves **to run** on the beach in bare feet.* ——→ Both sentences have exactly
*Martin loves **running** on the beach in bare feet.* the same meaning.

Some Common Verbs Followed by Gerunds or Infinitives				
start	like	prefer	begin	love
try	continue	hate	can't stand	

Some verbs can be followed by either a gerund or an infinitive, but there is a difference in meaning. Notice the difference in meaning:

*I <u>stopped</u> **to have** a cigarette yesterday.*   I stopped an activity to do something.

*I <u>stopped</u> **smoking** yesterday.*   I stopped doing something.

*Did you <u>remember</u> **to turn** off the fan?*   Did you remember to perform a task?

*I <u>remember</u> **seeing** him at the crime scene.*   I have a memory about something that happened in the past.

4. Prepositions Plus Gerunds

Many verbs have the structure verb + preposition + object. If the object is another verb, the second verb is a gerund.

*I'm excited **about travelling** to Greece.*

Certain verbs must have a noun or pronoun before the preposition.

Some Common Verbs Followed by Prepositions Plus Gerunds		
apologize for	fond of	look forward to
dream of	forgive **me** for	prevent **him** from
excited about	insist on	succeed in
feel like	interest in	think about

CLASS EXERCISE

Complete the sentence with the gerund or infinitive form of the verb. Simply write *to* before the verb or *ing* after it. In some instances, you may need to add a preposition before the gerund form.

Examples: Please forgive me **for (insult) ing** you.

Ovid appears eager **to (accept)** the deal.

1. My brother remembers   (hold)   me in his arms when I was a baby.

2. Please remember   (lock)   the doors when you leave.

3. We have finished   (make)   supper.

4. He is learning   (use)   a computer.

5. Mark is excited   (go)   to Florida.

6. Tony quit   (take)   drugs.

7. Be very careful. You don't want to risk   (catch)   a dangerous disease!

8. I like   (shop)   at that mall.

9. Would you mind   (help)   me lift this box?

10. You can't prevent her   (date)   that man.

11. I really miss   (spend)   time with my mother.

12. Jeremy's boss threatened   (fire)   him.

13. I promise   (rehire)   Jeremy.

14. My uncle is an alcoholic. He can't stop _____ (drink)

15. The students practiced _____ (pronounce) _____ the *r* sound.

16. My father is a handyman. He is used to _____ (work) _____ with his hands.

17. Do you really plan to stop _____ (bother) _____ him with those silly comments?

18. I really resent _____ (have) _____ to do almost all of the cleaning up around here.

19. She doesn't pretend _____ (speak) _____ Greek perfectly, but she does know enough to get by.

20. I don't think that his personality is worth _____ (discuss) _____ at this point.

21. I've arranged _____ (leave) _____ the keys with a neighbor.

22. My grandmother says that she has often regretted _____ (leave) _____ her homeland.

23. I'd like to apologize _____ (disturb) _____ your sleep.

24. Please stop _____ (stare) _____ at me. It makes me uncomfortable.

25. I'm thirsty. Could we stop _____ (buy) _____ a drink?

Appendix 3

Pronouns

Table of Pronouns					
	Subject	**Object**	**Possessive Adjective**	**Possessive Pronoun**	**Reflexive**
Singular	I	me	my	mine	myself
	you	you	your	yours	yourself
	he	him	his	his	himself
	she	her	her	hers	herself
	it	it	its		itself
Plural	we	us	our	ours	ourselves
	you	you	your	yours	yourselves
	they	them	their	theirs	themselves

Rule 1: When the pronoun refers to the subject of the sentence, use the subject pronoun, and when it refers to the object of the sentence, use the object pronoun.

> *In spite of the difficulty, Mark and **I** climbed the mountain.*   (subject pronoun)
>
> *You really should excuse yourself to the Bensons and **me**.*   (object pronoun)

Rule 2: Sometimes a pronoun appears at the end of the sentence, and you're not sure if you should use the subject or the object pronoun. When in doubt, complete the thought.

> *She has worked here longer than **(I / me)**.*
> Complete the thought: *She has worked here longer than I have.*
>
> *The car belongs to Jane as much as **(I / me)**.*
> Complete the thought: *The car belongs to Jane as much as it belongs to me.*

Rule 3: Use *reflexive pronouns* when the subject doing the action and the object receiving the action are the same.

> *The Smiths should help **themselves** to the coffee.*
>
> *He is very proud of **himself**.*

CLASS EXERCISE

Circle the correct answer.

1. After I had insulted the hostess, I asked (me / myself) why I had been so rude.

2. Calvin has to help (him / himself) to dinner.

3. Ronald is Anna's son. Anna is (his / her) mother.

4. Marley is Bob's wife. Bob is (his / her) husband.

5. Sara has two sons. Those two boys are (his / her / hers).

6. The Langs are reclusive. They keep to (they / theirselves / themselves).

7. Little Billy cleaned his room by (him / hisself / himself).

8. He seems to be under the impression that he was smarter than (I / me), just because he received better marks in school than (I / me).

9. Anne bakes much better than (I / me).

10. We bought (us / ourselves) a dog.

11. When (your / you're) young, you don't have a lot of experience.

12. If (your / you're) going to walk there, wear a scarf.

13. Every worker should do (his or her / their) best.

14. It looks like (their / they're / there) going to be late again.

15. Anne asked us to visit, but Joe and (me / I) couldn't make it.

16. If you give us a lift, Marc and (I / me) would appreciate it.

17. Theresa helps everybody else more than (I / me).

18. Nobody talks as much as (she / her).

19. If you believe in (you / yourself) anything is possible.

20. Why didn't you ask (me / myself) to help you?

Appendix 4

Communication Activities

Grammar is more easily absorbed by students if they have an opportunity to integrate grammar into their activities. If the students have readings, they could be encouraged to discuss and debate the points in the readings. If the students are in a course that focuses on grammar, then the following activities can get the students to practice using the grammar.

The following activities could be used with students of all levels. For example, the first game appears easy, but even high-intermediate level students are unfamiliar with some of the verbs listed.

1. GESTURES GAME

(Present and past tenses)
The teacher chooses about 15 of the words. Students are then told to act out the words. The teacher may have to model each gesture once if the vocabulary is all unfamiliar for the students. Students who don't understand the vocabulary at the beginning of the game should understand it at the end of the game.

Suggested Vocabulary

wink	kiss	sip	tear	peel	put out	grab
blink	snore	swallow	sweep	scrub	take off	shove
shrug	snort	rub	wipe	scrape	put on	shovel
sob	cough	sneer	grind	spread	put down	turn on
sigh	sneeze	frown	mash	slice	pick up	turn off
laugh	clap	grin	sponge	chop	pick at	
giggle	tap	pout	stir	sprinkle	take away	
hug	snap	whine	spill	put away	dent	

Questions could also be practiced with this game. As one student acts out a verb, another could ask what he or she is doing, or did.

2. MYSTERY VERB GAME

(Present and past tenses, question forms)

The student must choose a word from the above list. For example, the student may decide to use the word *hug*. The other students must question the first student to try to find the mystery verb. All questions must be yes/no style questions. For example, the students in the class may ask the following types of questions:

> *Do you blank every morning?*
>
> *Do you blank alone?*
>
> *Do you blank in the kitchen?*

Students use the word *blank* until they think that they have discovered the mystery verb. New verbs may be added to the list to make this game more challenging.

3. JOBS DISCUSSION

(Present, past and future tenses, modals)

Brainstorm a list of occupations on the board. Beside each occupation, list particular skills or qualities that are necessary for that type of job. Then, in a third column, write down the type of education that is needed for each job. Students can be encouraged to mention jobs that they have, or that their friends or family members have. Students can also think about their future ambitions, and their ideal jobs.

Example:

Occupation	Skills or Qualities	Education Needed
Doctor	Perseverance/Intelligence	University degree in medicine
	Ability to be emotionally detached	
	Ambition	
	Social skills (for effective interaction with patients)	

If the students have quite advanced vocabulary, find some more obscure jobs. For example: Primatologist, endocrinologist, etc.

Discuss which jobs are most likely to disappear in an increasingly computerized work place. Which jobs are probably the most stressful? Which jobs would be most difficult to combine with a family life?

4. RECREATE THE POSE

(Modals, imperatives)

Two students come to the front of the classroom and sit on chairs facing the same direction. Student A sits in front of Student B and cannot see Student B. Student B strikes, or is given, a relatively difficult pose. The students in the class must then give Student A directions so that he or she is in exactly the same pose as Student B. Students in the class are not allowed to indicate, with gestures, what the pose is. They must use language to describe the position of Student B.

5. TELL THE TRUTH

(All verb tenses, question forms)

Students must think up three stories about themselves. Two of the stories are true, and one is a lie. The other students must ask the first student very detailed questions to find out which story is the lie. Students must be very careful in their use of tenses, and the teacher should intervene if a student incorrectly forms a question. This activity should be modelled by the teacher first.

To encourage the students to participate, they could be given a point for each correct question. Therefore those who don't participate would get no points.

For example:

> I was an extra in a Paul Newman movie in 1985. (lie)
>
> I accidentally dropped a dictionary on my pet hamster when I was young. (true)
>
> I won $50 in a lottery last week. (true)

Possible questions:

> What is the name of the movie that you were in?
>
> How many hamsters have you owned in your life?
>
> Where did you buy last week's winning lottery ticket?

6. ROLE PLAYING SUGGESTIONS

One student should read a situation described below under the heading "Student A." The student's partner should read the same-numbered situation described under the heading "Student B." Both students then meet at the front of the class and role-play the situation.

Student A

1. You are interviewing a candidate for a job as a legal secretary. Ask the candidate about his or her salary requirements, family situation, reasons for wanting this job, skills, weaknesses and strengths, teamwork experience, and work experience. Be careful when you form questions. Make sure that you use the correct question word order. Because the job requires a lot of late hours, find out if the candidate can do overtime work.

2. You repair refrigerators. You come to fix someone's fridge. You very quickly change a small piece. The cost is $90. Be inflexible.

3. You are driving very quickly. When you are stopped for speeding, try to bribe the police officer.

4. You are sitting in an airplane. The passenger in front of you is smoking. Ask the passenger to stop smoking. You are asthmatic, and smoke is very bad for your health.

5. You are a teacher and your spouse is a lawyer. Your spouse has been offered a great job in Yellowknife. You don't want to go for many reasons.

6. You and your roommate found a mouse in the kitchen, and there is scratching behind the walls. You have also seen cockroaches in the kitchen. Explain the situation to the landlord. You would like the rent reduced because of these problems.

7. You go to the doctor. You often feel nauseous, and you have a headache and a sore throat. The doctor will explain what your ailment is. Refuse to take any antibiotics. Ask the doctor if he or she could suggest a homeopathic remedy, or a herbal tea. You don't believe in antibiotics.

8. Phone your child. You are 70 years old, and are not feeling very well. Your knees hurt, and lately you have been feeling faint. You are also very worried about your child's marriage. Lately your child has seemed very tense around his or her spouse, and they argue a lot. Try to get your child to talk about it. You are also upset because your grandchildren seem too thin. Maybe they aren't being fed enough. Make sure your child listens to you. After all, you went through 20 hours of labour to have that child!

Student B

1. You are being interviewed for a job as a legal secretary. Answer the interviewer's questions honestly. You really need this job because you are an unemployed single parent of three small children.

2. Your fridge doesn't defrost. A repair person comes to your door. The repair is done very quickly. You refuse to pay the bill because it is too high.

3. You are a police officer. Stop a motorist for speeding. Ask to see the motorist's identification papers.

4. You are in an airplane. You are enjoying a cigarette. When someone asks you to put it out, refuse. After all, the No Smoking light has been put out, and you are sitting in the smoking section.

5. You are a lawyer and your spouse is a teacher. You have just been offered a great job in Yellowknife, with a very high salary and very challenging work. You desperately want to go. You are bored and unmotivated in your present job, and really need the change. Convince your spouse to make the move.

6. You are the landlord of a very nice building. Two messy tenants make rather dubious complaints about their apartment. They are probably just trying to take advantage of your kind nature. Be firm with them. The other tenants in the building never have problems. Don't let these tenants get away with anything.

7. You are a doctor. Listen to a patient's complaints. After listening to the complaints, take a throat swab. The patient has severe strep throat and must go on antibiotics immediately. The infection could get much more serious without proper treatment, so make sure that the patient takes your advice. Write out a prescription.

8. Your mother calls. You feel quite tired after a long day of work, and you really just want to relax for a few minutes and read the newspaper before the kids get home from school. Soon you and your spouse have to prepare the evening meal. Be polite to your mother, but do let her know that you can't talk for long.

Appendix 5

Table of Irregular Verbs

Base Form	Simple Past	Past Participle	Base Form	Simple Past	Past Participle
Arise	Arose	Arisen	Do	Did	Done
Be	Was, were	Been	Draw	Drew	Drawn
Bear	Bore	Borne	Drink	Drank	Drunk
Beat	Beat	Beaten	Drive	Drove	Driven
Become	Became	Become	Eat	Ate	Eaten
Begin	Began	Begun	Fall	Fell	Fallen
Bend	Bent	Bent	Feed	Fed	Fed
Bet	Bet	Bet	Fight	Fought	Fought
Bind	Bound	Bound	Find	Found	Found
Bite	Bit	Bitten	Flee	Fled	Fled
Bleed	Bled	Bled	Fly	Flew	Flown
Blow	Blew	Blown	Forbid	Forbade	Forbidden
Break	Broke	Broken	Forget	Forgot	Forgotten
Bring	Brought	Brought	Forgive	Forgave	Forgiven
Build	Built	Built	Forsake	Forsook	Forsaken
Burst	Burst	Burst	Freeze	Froze	Frozen
Buy	Bought	Bought	Get	Got	Got, gotten
Catch	Caught	Caught	Give	Gave	Given
Choose	Chose	Chosen	Go	Went	Gone
Cling	Clung	Clung	Grind	Ground	Ground
Come	Came	Come	Grow	Grew	Grown
Cost	Cost	Cost	Hang	Hung	Hung
Creep	Crept	Crept	Have	Had	Had
Cut	Cut	Cut	Hear	Heard	Heard
Dig	Dug	Dug	Hide	Hid	Hidden

Base Form	Simple Past	Past Participle	Base Form	Simple Past	Past Participle
Hit	Hit	Hit	Sing	Sang	Sung
Hold	Held	Held	Sink	Sank	Sunk
Hurt	Hurt	Hurt	Sit	Sat	Sat
Keep	Kept	Kept	Sleep	Slept	Slept
Know	Knew	Known	Slide	Slid	Slid
Lay	Laid	Laid	Speak	Spoke	Spoken
Lead	Led	Led	Speed	Sped	Sped
Leave	Left	Left	Spend	Spent	Spent
Lend	Lent	Lent	Spin	Spun	Spun
Let	Let	Let	Split	Split	Split
Lie	Lay	Lain	Spread	Spread	Spread
Light	Lit	Lit	Spring	Sprang	Sprung
Lose	Lost	Lost	Stand	Stood	Stood
Make	Made	Made	Steal	Stole	Stolen
Mean	Meant	Meant	Stick	Stuck	Stuck
Meet	Met	Met	Sting	Stung	Stung
Pay	Paid	Paid	Stink	Stank	Stunk
Prove	Proved	Proved/Proven	Strike	Struck	Struck
Put	Put	Put	Swear	Swore	Sworn
Quit	Quit	Quit	Sweep	Swept	Swept
Read	Read	Read	Swim	Swam	Swum
Rid	Rid	Rid	Swing	Swung	Swung
Ride	Rode	Ridden	Take	Took	Taken
Ring	Rang	Rung	Teach	Taught	Taught
Rise	Rose	Risen	Tear	Tore	Torn
Run	Ran	Run	Tell	Told	Told
Say	Said	Said	Think	Thought	Thought
See	Saw	Seen	Throw	Threw	Thrown
Sell	Sold	Sold	Thrust	Thrust	Thrust
Send	Sent	Sent	Understand	Understood	Understood
Set	Set	Set	Upset	Upset	Upset
Shake	Shook	Shaken	Wake	Woke	Woken
Shine	Shone	Shone	Wear	Wore	Worn
Shoot	Shot	Shot	Weep	Wept	Wept
Show	Showed	Shown	Win	Won	Won
Shrink	Shrank	Shrunk	Wind	Wound	Wound
Shut	Shut	Shut	Withdraw	Withdrew	Withdrawn

Appendix 6

Essay Writing Summary

You may be called upon to write formal or informal essays. If you write a narrative essay about a personal experience, then your writing style can be informal. However, if you are asked to write a more formal opinion essay, there are certain rules you should follow.

- **Avoid using contractions.** Instead of *I don't*, you should write *I do not*.

- **Avoid slang expressions.** For example: If you dislike a movie, do not write: *"The movie sucks."* Make sure that the level of language is appropriate.

- **Avoid using the personal pronoun "I."** In some opinion essays it is appropriate to support your point of view with references to your own experiences. For example, in the essay "Women on the Road" (on page 32 of this book) the writer illustrates her point of view with examples from her own travelling experiences, so she uses the personal pronoun "I."

The essay "Disadvantages of Being a Teen Parent" (on page 49 of this book) is a more formal essay, and the writer never refers to herself. However, if the writer were a teen parent, she could convincingly support her point of view by referring to personal experiences, thus necessitating the use of "I."

Structuring an Opinion Essay

Before you write your opinion essay, make an essay plan. Make sure that your essay is well structured. Your completed essay should include the following elements:

The Introduction

Am introduction should arouse the reader's interest in the topic. If your introduction is very boring, and you simply list your reasons for your opinion, you take the punch out of your essay. Try to introduce your topic in an interesting, creative way. Making a controversial statement is one way to get the reader's attention. However, there are many other ways to stimulate the reader's interest and at the same time draw the reader into your argument. You could begin your essay with an anecdote, you could describe something related to the topic, or you could give historical background information.

When you think about a subject, decide what your point of view is and state your point of view in a **thesis statement**. A thesis statement is a general opinion statement, and no reasons for the opinion need to be given in this statement.

The Body Paragraphs

A good **topic sentence** introduces the subject of the paragraph and gets the reader's attention. The point that you are trying to make in your paragraph should be clearly evident in an interesting topic sentence. Everything else in the paragraph should be a detail that supports your topic sentence.

To guide the reader from one idea to the next, or from one paragraph to the next, use **transitional words or phrases** that smoothly link one idea to another. For a comprehensive list of transitional words and phrases, see the WRITING TIPS section in Chapter 8.

Each body paragraph should be developed with **supporting facts and examples.** Remember, the facts and examples should be directly related to the topic sentence (focus sentence) of the paragraph.

The Conclusion

In the conclusion, remind the reader of the thesis of the essay as well as the main supporting points. End your conclusion creatively with a final comment. You could make a prediction or a suggestion. You could also end with a surprising statement that gives your essay a final punch.

Technical Errors Suggestion

Each time your teacher corrects your essay, the teacher indicates your spelling and grammatical errors. You probably have some bad habits and your bad habits will remain unless you attempt to retrain yourself. In order to avoid making the same mistakes over and over, you could prepare an "Errors cheat sheet." On this sheet you can record a list of your errors. You can also write down rules for your major grammatical problems, and include examples from your essays.

After receiving a corrected essay, your "Errors Cheat Sheet" could look like this:

Errors "Cheat Sheet"

Number of errors

3 spelling mistakes

6 subject-verb agreement

3 verb tense

2 incorrect word choice

Spelling list

wich > which

responsable > responsible

beleive > believe

Grammar Problem #1:	Subject-verb agreement
Rule:	Add "s" or "es" to all third-person singular present tense verbs.
Examples:	This situation *provides* them with an excuse to be violent.
	The solution to this problem *remains* unclear.
Grammar Problem #2:	Verb tense (Shifting from past to present tense)

You could refer to this cheat sheet the each time you write an essay, and you could make a new sheet after each essay. In time, you will train yourself to stop repeating the same mistakes.

Good luck with your essay writing!

Grammar Index

Literary Credits

p. 1 "Carnival of Carnivores" by Joe Fiorito, from *Comfort Me With Apples,* published by Nuage Editions. Reprinted with permission.

p. 8 "Friends all of us" by Pablo Neruda, from *Neruda and Vallejo: Selected Poems*, edited by Robert Bly, Beacon Press, Boston, 1971, 1993. © Copyright 1971, 1993 by Robert Bly. Reprinted with his permission.

p. 10 "First Steps" by Adele Berridge. Reprinted with permission.

p. 16 "It's Called Children's Entertainment" by Gwynne Dyer, from *The Montreal Gazette*, December 15, 1995, p. B3. Reprinted with permission of the author.

p. 25 "Where are you going, kid?" condensed from *Portraits de Sarajevo* by Zlatko Dizdarevic. (Publié par Editions Spengler, Paris, 1994). From *Reader's Digest* (Canada) January 1996, p. 66. Reprinted with permission.

p. 34 "The Appalling Truth" by Dorothy Nixon. Reprinted with permission.

p. 43 "Why We Crave Horror Movies" by Stephen King. Reprinted with permission. © Stephen King. All rights reserved.

p. 52 "Shame" from *Nigger: An Autobiography* by Dick Gregory. Copyright © 1964 by Dick Gregory Enterprises, Inc. Used by permission of Dutton Signet, a division of Penguin Books USA Inc.

p. 59 "Mission Improbable," *People Weekly*, March 11, 1996. Susan Reed, Cathy Nolan/*People Weekly* © 1996 Time Inc.

p. 66 "Bad News About the Effects of Divorce" by Lloyd Billingsley. Appeared in *Christianity Today*, © 1982. Reprinted with permission of author.

p. 70 "The Starvation Demons" by Adrienne Webb, *Maclean's*, May 2, 1994. Reprinted with permission.

p. 76 "The Preoccupation with Tears" by Charles Gordon, *Maclean's*, July 22, 1985. Reprinted with permission.

p. 80 "Biceps in a Bottle" by James Deacon, *Maclean's,* May 2, 1994. Reprinted with permission.

p. 84 "The Body Builders" by Patricia Chisolm, *Maclean's*, July 8, 1996. Reprinted with permission.

p. 95 "Versions" by Genni Gunn, from *The Journey Prize Anthology* (McClelland & Stewart, 1993), © Genni Gunn. Reprinted with permission of the author.

p. 103 "The Premeditated Death of Samuel Glover" by Hugh Garner, from *The Yellow Sweater and Other Stories* (Toronto: William Collins and Sons, 1953). Reprinted with permission of McGraw-Hill Ryerson Limited.